The Contemporaries Meet the Classics on Prayer

✳

THE
CONTEMPORARIES
MEET
THE CLASSICS
ON
PRAYER

*

From the writings of such authors as

HENRI NOUWEN, MARTIN LUTHER, TONY EVANS,

OSWALD CHAMBERS, STORMIE OMARTIAN,

CHARLES H. SPURGEON, & MANY MORE

COMPILED BY LEONARD ALLEN, PH.D

Our purpose at Howard Publishing is to:

- *Increase faith* in the hearts of growing Christians
- *Inspire holiness* in the lives of believers
- *Instill hope* in the hearts of struggling people everywhere
  Because He's coming again!

The Contemporaries Meet the Classics on Prayer © 2003 Compiled by Leonard Allen
All rights reserved. Printed in the United States of America
Published by Howard Publishing Co., Inc.
3117 North 7th Street, West Monroe, Louisiana 71291-2227
In association with the literary agency of Alive Communications, Inc.
7680 Goddard Street, Suite 200, Colorado Springs, CO 80920

03 04 05 06 07 08 09 10 11 12   10 9 8 7 6 5 4 3 2

Edited by Julie Meredith
Interior design by John Luke
Cover design by David Carlson, David Carlson Design
Cover illustration by Nicholas Wilton

Library of Congress Cataloging-in-Publication Data

The contemporaries meet the classics on prayer / from the writings of Max Lucado ... [et al.] ; compiled by Leonard Allen.
    p. cm.
   ISBN 978-1-4767-4107-9
   1. Prayer—Christianity. I. Lucado, Max. II. Allen, Crawford Leonard.

BV210.3.C66 2003
248.3'2—dc21

                                                          2002191346

Editorial Note: Mistakes in grammar and punctuation that were inherent in the original source were not corrected. Multiple Bible versions were used by the various authors included in this work. Some were noted by the authors; others were not. Known versions are listed on this page with permission-to-use notations. Scriptures on pages facing chapter openings are from the HOLY BIBLE, NEW INTERNATIONAL VERSION®. Copyright© 1973, 1978, 1984 by International Bible Society. Used by permission of Zondervan Publishing House. All rights reserved. Scriptures marked NASB taken from the NEW AMERICAN STANDARD BIBLE®, Copyright © 1960, 1962, 1963, 1971, 1972, 1973, 1975, 1977, 1995 by The Lockman Foundation. Used by permission.

CONTENTS

✸

Contents

INTRODUCTION

✷

"Prayer catapults us onto the frontier of the spiritual life. Of all the Spiritual Disciplines prayer is the most central because it ushers us into perpetual communion with the Father."

—Richard Foster, *Celebration of Discipline*

"The prayers of God's saints are the capital stock in heaven by which Christ carries on His great work upon earth."

—E. M. Bounds, *Purpose in Prayer*

"Prayer is for us to confess, weep for our tragic state. As children unburden their troubles to their parents, so it is with us before God."

—John Calvin, *Institutes of the Christian Religion*

Prayer is the lifeline of the Christian faith. To become a Christian and enter the community of faith is to learn the practice of prayer. The church is a school of prayer. There we find the mothers and fathers who pray with their children, the elders who pray for the sick, the pastors who pray for their flocks, the psalmists of Israel with their inspired words for prayer, the saints across the ages who left us the stories and records of their praying. These are all our teachers—faithfully speaking the language of prayer, modeling for us the practice of prayer, and insisting that we too join them in the great lineage of prayers.

This book is an anthology of the church's rich and varied tradition of prayer. It draws upon the experiences and insights of contemporary writers (those writing since 1950), then sets alongside them earlier writers (mainly from 1500 forward) whose works have shown the quality and staying power of classics. Three purposes have guided the building of this collection:

1. *Encouraging a fuller, richer prayer life for Christians.* Who could read Martin Luther's bold advice to the new "protestants" of his day, and not be stirred by the privilege of prayer? Or Andrew Murray's call to enter into Christ's school of prayer and not be challenged to greater faith? Or Jonathan Edwards's account of his "vehement longing for God" and not be emboldened by his passion? Or Rosalind Rinker's simple way to pray with others and not be encouraged to seek new prayer relationships? The faith we observe through the eyes of others' experiences with effective prayer reinforces and reminds us of our own belief in the power that is ours through prayer.

2. *Expanding our understanding of the historic tradition of prayer.* In that tradition one discovers, for example, the foundational role of the Psalms in prayer—a role long honored in the Christian tradition. Through the ages Christians have viewed the Psalms as God's prayer book—a divinely given guide for cultivating fluency in prayer. So in morning prayer, according to the traditional practice, one doesn't just pray whatever one happens to feel but rather is directed by God's inspired prayer book. Then, at later times during the day, one prays; not the psalmists' prayers themselves, but *like* the psalmists—that is, out of one's own elation or trial or temptation fresh prayers flow. As our understanding of the great tradition of Christian prayer grows, our own prayer lives are enriched and deepened.

3. *Recovering dimensions of prayer that may have been neglected in contemporary Christian traditions as well as discovering insights from those in recent years less bound by tradition.* For example, the practice of *lecto divino,* or holy reading—a classic method of using Scripture in prayer—remains foreign to many Christians today; to discover it is to find an effective and time-honored tool used in spiritual formation throughout Christian history. Those seeking a more personal relationship with God can benefit from contemporary Christians whose experience of God through conversational prayer and listening prayer journals has brought them to greater intimacy with Him. The Christian heritage of prayer—both contemporary and classic—is full of

insights just waiting to be discovered and appropriated for our use today.

Prayer is the natural, original language of human beings. Many things in our lives stifle and inhibit that language, but it is our most basic human language. In the Christian community we are taught that language—by saints new and old, by pastors and friends, in brokenness and healing, in secret and in public.

We pray because God invites us to pray. God invites us to speak with Him, bringing our praise and thanksgiving, our confession of sin, our wounds and hurts, our supplications for others, our own perceived needs—everything that concerns us. So "let us therefore draw near with confidence to the throne of grace, that we may receive mercy and may find grace to help in time of need" (Heb. 4:16 NASB). I pray that this book will bless and encourage you to draw near the throne.

LEONARD ALLEN

PRAYER

DO NOT BE ANXIOUS ABOUT ANYTHING, BUT IN
EVERYTHING, BY PRAYER AND PETITION, WITH
THANKSGIVING, PRESENT YOUR REQUESTS TO GOD.
AND THE PEACE OF GOD, WHICH TRANSCENDS ALL
UNDERSTANDING, WILL GUARD YOUR HEARTS AND
YOUR MINDS IN CHRIST JESUS.

PHILIPPIANS 4:6–7

PRAY IN THE SPIRIT ON ALL OCCASIONS WITH ALL
KINDS OF PRAYERS AND REQUESTS....BE ALERT AND
ALWAYS KEEP ON PRAYING FOR ALL THE SAINTS.

EPHESIANS 6:18

DEVOTE YOURSELVES TO PRAYER, BEING WATCHFUL
AND THANKFUL.

COLOSSIANS 4:2

CHAPTER I

THE
PURPOSE
OF
PRAYER

❈

Why Should We Pray?
OLE HALLESBY — 1931

To many this problem seems easy to solve. We should pray, they say, in order to get God to give us something!

So simple does it appear to them.

But a moment's reflection will convince us that this view of prayer is pagan and not Christian. We all have so much of the pagan left in us that it is easy for us to look upon prayer as a means whereby we can make God kind and good, and grant our prayer. But the whole revelation of God teaches us that this is to misunderstand both God and prayer completely.

God is in Himself good, from eternity and to eternity; He was good before humanity had any occasion for prayer. The Scriptures also teach us that God is equally kind and good whether He grants our prayers or not. When he grants our prayers, it is because He loves us. When He does not, it is also because He loves us.

Others say, "No, the purpose of prayer is to tell God what we need."

But neither is this solution adequate to the problem involved in Christian prayer. By the revelation of God we Christians are convinced that as far as God is concerned it is not at all necessary for us to explain our needs to Him. On the contrary, God alone fully understands what each one of us needs; we make mistakes continually and pray for things which would be harmful to us if we received them. Afterwards we see our mistakes and realize that God is good and wise in not giving us these things, even though we plead ever so earnestly for them.

But this again throws us into a quandary as to why we should pray at all.

If God gives us His gifts of His own accord, and if He does not need to be told by us what to give, why should we pray at all?

This question is not one of mere theoretical interest. It is one of great practical importance because of the way it affects our views both of God and of prayer. The question is in reality this: Why does not God give us His gifts before we pray, even without our prayer, since He is Himself good, and since it is His will to give us these things, and since He does not need any suggestions from us?

In answering this question, we must take as our starting point the words of Jesus in Matthew 5:45, "He maketh his sun to rise on the evil and on the good, and sendeth rain on the just and on the unjust." In these words Jesus reveals clearly that aspect of God's perfect love according to which He gives everybody all that He can persuade them, in one way or another, to accept.

"On the evil and on the good," says Jesus. The evil do not ask Him for it, but He gives it to them nevertheless. The good ask, to be sure; but if they did not receive more than they prayed for, they would not receive very much. Hence both have this in common, that they receive a great deal from God without asking for it.

Why do they receive these things without asking?

Simply because God is love. And *the essence of love is to give:* give all it has to give, give all it can give without bringing harm to the loved one, give all it can persuade the loved one to accept.

That God gives some gifts to people without their prayer and other gifts only to those who pray, can be accounted for by the simple fact that there is a wide difference in kind between these gifts.

All people accept some of God's gifts; this is true, for instance, of temporal gifts. They are given without our prayer.

But we close our hearts to some of God's other gifts; this is true of all the gifts which pertain to our salvation. These gifts God cannot bestow upon us before He can persuade us to open our hearts and receive them voluntarily. And, as we have seen above, prayer is the organ whereby we open our hearts to God and let Him enter in.

Here we see why prayer is essential.

It is not for the purpose of making God good or generous. He is that from all eternity.

Nor is it for the purpose of informing God concerning our needs. He knows what they are better than we do. Nor is it for the purpose of bringing God's gifts down from heaven to us. It is He who bestows the gifts, and by knocking at the door of our hearts, He reminds us that He desires to impart them to us.

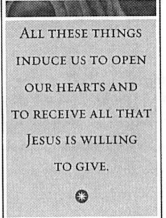

ALL THESE THINGS INDUCE US TO OPEN OUR HEARTS AND TO RECEIVE ALL THAT JESUS IS WILLING TO GIVE.

No, prayer has one function, and that is to answer "Yes," when He knocks, to open the soul and give Him the opportunity to bring us the answer.

This throws light on the struggles and strivings, the work and the fasting connected with prayer. All these things have but one purpose: to induce us to open our hearts and to receive all that Jesus is willing to give, to put away all those things which would distract us and prevent us from hearing Jesus knock, that is, from hearing the Spirit of prayer when He tries to tell us what God is waiting to give us if we will only ask for it.

OLE HALLESBY (1879–1961) was a Norwegian Lutheran pastor and professor of theology at the Free Faculty of Theology in Oslo, Norway. His writings in English translation include the classic *Prayer and Temperament and the Christian Faith.*

The Chief End of Prayer
ANDREW MURRAY – 1895

'I go unto the Father. And whatsoever ye shall ask in my Name, that will I do, that the Father may be glorified in the Son.' —John xiv.13.

That the Father may be glorified in the Son: it is to this end that Jesus on His throne in glory will do all we ask in His Name. Every answer to prayer He gives will have this as its object: when there is no prospect of this object being obtained, He will not answer. It follows as a matter of course that this must be with us, as with Jesus, the essential element in our petitions: the glory of the Father must be the aim and end, the very soul and life of our prayer.

It was so with Jesus when He was on earth. 'I seek not mine own honour: I seek the honour of Him that sent me;' in such words we have the keynote of His life. In the first words of the high priestly prayer He gives utterance to it: 'Father! glorify Thy son, *that Thy Son may glorify Thee. I have glorified Thee* on earth; glorify me with Thyself.' The ground on which He asks to be taken up into the glory He had with the Father, is the twofold one: He has glorified Him on earth; He will still glorify Him in heaven. What He asks is only to enable Him to glorify the Father more. It is as we enter into sympathy with Jesus on this point, and gratify Him by making the Father's glory our chief object in prayer too, that our prayer cannot fail of an answer. There is nothing of which the Beloved Son has said more distinctly that it will glorify the Father than this, His doing what we ask; He will not, therefore, let any opportunity slip of securing this object. Let us make His aim ours: let the glory of the Father be the link between our asking and His doing: such prayer must prevail.

This word of Jesus comes indeed as a sharp two-edged sword, piercing even to the dividing of soul and spirit, and quick to discern the thoughts and intents of the heart. Jesus in His prayers on earth, in His intercession in heaven, in His promise of an answer to our prayers from there, makes this His first object—the glory of His Father. Is it so with us too? Or are not, in large measure, self-interest and self-will the strongest motives urging us to pray? Or, if we cannot see that this is the case, have we not to acknowledge that the distinct, conscious longing for the glory of the Father is not what animates our prayers? And yet it must be so.

Not as if the believer does not at times desire it. But he has to mourn that he has so little attained. And he knows the reason of his failure too. It was, because the separation between the spirit of daily life and the spirit of the hour of prayer was too wide. We begin to see that the desire for the glory of the Father is not something that we can awake and present to our Lord when we prepare ourselves to pray. No! it is only when the whole life, in all its parts, is given up to God's glory, that we can really pray to His glory too. '*Do all* to the glory of God,' and, '*Ask all* to the glory of God,'—these twin commands are inseparable: obedience to the former is the secret of grace for the latter. A life to the glory of God is the condition of the prayers that Jesus can answer, 'that the Father may be glorified.'

This demand in connection with prevailing prayer—that it should be to the glory of God—is no more than right and natural. There is none glorious but the Lord: there is no glory but His, and what He layeth on His creatures. Creation exists to show forth His glory; all that is not for His glory is sin, and darkness, and death: it is only in the glorifying of God that the creatures can find glory. What the Son of Man did, to give Himself wholly, His whole life, to glorify the Father, is nothing but the simple duty of every redeemed one. And Christ's reward will be his too. Because He gave Himself so entirely to the glory of the Father, the Father crowned Him with glory and honour, giving the kingdom into His hands, with the power to ask what He will, and, as Intercessor, to answer our prayers. And just as we become one with Christ in this, and as our prayer is part of a life utterly surrendered to God's glory, will the Savior be able to glorify the Father to us by the fulfillment of the promise: 'Whatsoever ye shall ask, *I will do it.*'

To such a life, with God's glory our only aim, we cannot attain by any effort of our own. It is only in the man Christ Jesus that such a life is to be seen: in Him it is to be found for us. Yes, blessed be God! His life is our life; He gave *Himself* for us; He Himself is now our life. The discovery, and the confession, and the denial, of self, as usurping the place of God, of self-seeking and self-trusting, is essential, and yet is what we cannot accomplish in our own strength. It is the incoming and indwelling, the Presence and the Rule in the heart, of our Lord Jesus who glorified the Father on earth, and is now glorified with Him, that thence He might glorify Him in us;—it is Jesus Himself coming in, who can cast out all self-glorifying, and give us instead His own God-glorifying life and Spirit. It is Jesus, who longs to glorify the Father in hearing our prayers, who will teach us to live and to pray to the glory of God.

Andrew Murray (1828–1917) was born in South Africa, where he served as a missionary pastor for many years. His devotional writings include *The Believer's Prayer Life*, *Waiting on God*, and *The Blood of Christ*, which have become classics of the modern era.

True Prayer
John Bunyan – 1675

God commands us to pray. He commands us to pray in public and in private. Prayer brings those who have the spirit of supplication into a wonderful communion and fellowship with God; therefore, God has ordained prayer as a means for us to grow in a personal relationship with Him.

When we pray often and actively, our prayers acquire great

things from God, both for those for whom we pray as well as for ourselves. Prayer opens our heart to God. Our prayers are the means by which our souls, though empty, are filled by God to overflowing. In our prayers, we Christians can open our hearts to God as to a friend, and obtain a fresh confirmation of His friendship with us.

I might spend many words in distinguishing between public and private prayer. I might also distinguish between prayer in the heart and prayer that is spoken aloud. Something also might be said regarding the differences between the gifts and the graces of prayer. But I have chosen to make it my business to show you only the very heart of prayer, without which all your lifting up, both of hands and eyes and voices, will be to no purpose at all....

Prayer is a sincere, sensible, affectionate pouring out of the heart or soul to God, through Christ, in the strength and assistance of the Holy Spirit, for such things as God has promised, or according to the Word of God, for the good of the Church, with submission in faith to the will of God.

The definition includes seven things:...First, your prayers must be sincere. Second, your prayers must be sensible. Third, your prayers must be an affectionate pouring out of your soul to God the Father through Jesus Christ. Fourth, if you want your prayers to be effective, you must pray by the strength and assistance of the Holy Spirit. Fifth, for your prayers to be answered according to the will of God, you must pray for such things as God has promised, or according to His Word, the Bible. Sixth, your prayers should not be selfish, but should keep in view the good of the Church as well as others. Seventh, you should always pray in faith and with submission to the will of God.

JOHN BUNYAN (1628–1688) was a Puritan preacher and writer born in England. During his twelve-year imprisonment in a Bedford jail, he wrote *Pilgrim's Progress,* which has become one of the most widely read Christian works of all time.

The Main Business of Life
RICHARD FOSTER—1988

Prayer catapults us onto the frontier of the spiritual life. Of all the Spiritual Disciplines prayer is the most central because it ushers us into perpetual communion with the Father. Meditation introduces us to the inner life, fasting is an accompanying means, study transforms our minds, but it is the Discipline of prayer that brings us into the deepest and highest work of the human spirit. Real prayer is life creating and life changing. "Prayer—secret, fervent, believing prayer—lies at the root of all personal godliness," writes William Carey.

To pray is to change. Prayer is the central avenue God uses to transform us. If we are unwilling to change, we will abandon prayer as a noticeable characteristic of our lives. The closer we come to the heartbeat of God the more we see our need and the more we desire to be conformed to Christ. William Blake tells us that our task in life is to learn to bear God's "beams of love." How often we fashion cloaks of evasion—beam-proof shelters—in order to elude our Eternal Lover. But when we pray, God slowly and graciously reveals to us our evasive actions and sets us free from them.

"You ask and do not receive, because you ask wrongly, to spend it on your passions" (James 4:3). To ask "rightly" involves transformed passions. In prayer, real prayer, we begin to think God's thoughts after him: to desire the things he desires, to love the things he loves, to will the things he wills. Progressively, we are taught to see things from his point of view.

All who have walked with God have viewed prayer as the main business of their lives. The words of the gospel of Mark, "And in the morning, a great while before day, he rose and went out to a lonely place, and there he prayed," stand as a commentary on the life-style of Jesus (Mark 1:35). David's desire for God broke the self-indulgent chains of sleep: "Early will I seek Thee" (Ps. 63:1, KJV). When the apostles were tempted to invest their energies in other important and necessary tasks, they determined to give themselves continually to prayer and the ministry of the word (Acts 6:4). Martin Luther declares, "I have so much business I cannot get on without spending three hours daily in prayer." He held it as a spiritual axiom that "He that has prayed well has studied well." John Wesley says, "God does nothing but in answer to prayer," and backed up his conviction by devoting two hours daily to that sacred exercise. The most notable feature of David Brainerd's life was his praying. His Journal is permeated with accounts of prayer, fasting, and meditation. "I love to be alone in my cottage, where I can spend much time in prayer." "I set apart this day for secret fasting and prayer to God."

For those explorers in the frontiers of faith, prayer was no little habit tacked onto the periphery of their lives; it *was* their lives. It was the most serious work of their most productive years. William Penn testified of George Fox that "Above all he excelled in prayer....The most awful, living, reverend frame I ever felt or beheld, I must say was his in prayer." Adoniram Judson sought to withdraw from business and company seven times a day in order to engage in the holy work of prayer. He began at dawn; then at nine, twelve, three, six, nine, and midnight he would give time to secret prayer. John Hyde of India made prayer such a dominant characteristic of his life that he was nicknamed "Praying Hyde." For these, and all those who have braved the depths of the interior life, to breathe was to pray.

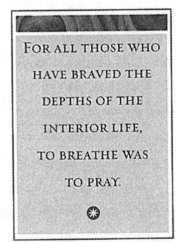

FOR ALL THOSE WHO HAVE BRAVED THE DEPTHS OF THE INTERIOR LIFE, TO BREATHE WAS TO PRAY.

RICHARD FOSTER is the founder of Renovare, a ministry of church renewal, and the author of *Celebration of Discipline, Freedom of Simplicity,* and other works. He presently serves as professor of spiritual formation at Azusa Pacific University in Southern California.

The Heart of the Life of Prayer
EVELYN UNDERHILL — 1926

Take first then, as primary, the achievement and maintenance of a right attitude toward God; that profound and awestruck sense of God's transcendent reality, that humbly adoring relation, on which all else depends. I feel no doubt that, for all who take the spiritual life seriously, this prayer of adoration exceeds all other types in educational and purifying power. It alone is able to consolidate our sense of the supernatural, to conquer our persistent self-occupation, to expand our spirits, to feed and quicken our awareness of the wonder and delightfulness of God.

There are two movements that must be plainly present in every complete spiritual life. The energy of its prayer must be directed on the one hand towards God; and on the other toward people. The first movement embraces the whole range of spiritual communion between the soul and God; in it we turn toward Divine Reality in adoration, bathing, so to speak, our souls in the Eternal Light. In the second we return, with the added peace and energy thus gained, to the natural world; there to do spiritual work for and with God for others. Thus prayer, like the whole of our inner life, "swings between the unseen and the seen." Now both these movements are of course necessary in all Christians; but the point is that the second will only be well done where the first has the central place. The deepening of the soul's unseen attachments must precede the outward swing toward the world in order to safeguard it.

This means that adoration, and not intercession or petition, must be the very heart of the life of prayer. For prayer is a supernatural activity or nothing at all; and it must primarily be directed to supernatural ends. It, too, acknowledges the soul's basic law: It comes from God, belongs to God, is destined for God. It must begin, end, and be enclosed in the atmosphere of adoration, aiming at God for and in God's self. Our ultimate effect as transmitters of heavenly light and love directly depends on this adoring attentiveness. In such a prayer of adoring attentiveness, we open our doors wide to receive God's ever-present Spirit; abasing ourselves and acknowledging our own nothingness. Only the soul that has thus given itself to God becomes part of the mystical body through which God acts on life. Its destiny is to be the receiver and transmitter of grace.

Is not that practical work? For Christians, surely, the only practical work. But sometimes we are in such a hurry to transmit that we forget our primary duty is to receive; and that God's self-imparting through us, will be in direct proportion to our adoring love and humble receptiveness. Only when our souls are filled to the brim, can we presume to offer spiritual gifts to others. The remedy for that sense of impotence, that desperate spiritual exhaustion that religious workers too often know, is, I am sure, an inner life governed not by petition but by adoring prayer. When we find that the demands made upon us are seriously threatening our inward poise, when we feel symptoms of starvation and stress, we can be quite sure that it is time to call a halt, to reestablish the fundamental relation of our souls with Eternal Reality, the Home and Father of our spirits. "Our hearts shall have no rest except in you." It is only when our hearts are thus actually at rest in God, in peaceful and self-oblivious adoration, that we can hope to show God's attractiveness to others.

In the flood tide of such adoring prayer, the soul is released from the strife and confusions of temporal life; it is lifted far beyond all petty controversies, petty worries, and petty vanities—and none of us escape these things. It is carried into God, hidden in God. This is the only way in which it can achieve the utter self-forgetfulness that is the basis of its peace and power and that can never be ours as long as we make our prayer primarily a means of drawing gifts to ourselves and others from God, instead of an act of unmeasured self-giving.

I am certain that we gradually and imperceptibly learn more about God by this persistent attitude of humble adoration than we can hope to do by any amount of mental exploration. For in it our soul recaptures, if only for a moment, the fundamental relation of the tiny created spirit with its Eternal Source....In it we breathe deeply the atmosphere of Eternity; and when we do that, humility and common sense are found to be the same thing. We realize, and re-realize, our tininess, our nothingness, and the greatness and steadfastness of God. And we all know how priceless such a realization is for those who have to face the grave spiritual risk of presuming to teach others about God....

Thus it is surely of the first importance for those who are called to exacting lives of service to determine that nothing shall interfere with the development and steady, daily practice of loving and adoring prayer, a prayer full of intimacy and awe. It alone maintains the soul's energy and peace, and checks the temptation to leave God for God's service. I think that if you have only as little as half an hour to give each morning to your private prayer, it is not too much to make up your minds to spend half that time in such adoration. For it is the central service asked by God of human souls; and its neglect is responsible for much lack of spiritual depth and power. Moreover, it is more deeply refreshing, pacifying, and assuring than any other type of prayer. But only those know this who are practiced in adoring love.

EVELYN UNDERHILL (1875–1941) was a British writer and spiritual director. Her books *Mysticism* and *Worship* are her best-known works. In 1924 she began to conduct retreats, and a number of her books grew out of these conferences. For selections from her writings, see *An Anthology of the Love of God: From the Writings of Evelyn Underhill,* ed. Lumsden Barkway (1953).

The Testimony of George Muller
GEORGE MULLER—*1896*

I had constantly cases brought before me, which proved that one of the especial things which the children of God needed in our day, was *to have their faith strengthened.*

I longed, therefore, to have something to point my brethren to as a visible proof that our God and Father is the same faithful God as ever He was; as willing as ever to PROVE Himself to be the LIVING GOD in our day as formerly, *to all who put their trust in Him.*

My spirit longed to be instrumental in strengthening their faith, by giving them not only instances from the word of God, of His willingness and ability to help all who rely upon Him, but to *show them* by proofs that He is the same in our day. I knew that the word of God ought to be enough, and it was by grace enough for me; but still I considered I ought to lend a helping hand to my brethren.

I therefore judged myself bound to be the servant of the Church of Christ, in the particular point in which I had obtained mercy; namely, in being able to take God at His word and rely upon it. The first object of the work was, and is still: *that God might be magnified* by the fact that the orphans under my care are provided with all they need, *only by prayer and faith,* without any one being asked; thereby it may be seen that God is FAITHFUL STILL, AND HEARS PRAYER STILL.

I have again these last days prayed much about the Orphan House, and have frequently examined my heart; that if it were at all my desire to establish it for the sake of gratifying myself, I might find it out. For as I desire only the Lord's glory, I shall be glad to be instructed by the instrumentality of my brother, if the matter be not of Him.

When I began the Orphan work in 1835, my chief object was the glory of God, by giving a practical demonstration as to what could be accomplished simply through the instrumentality of prayer and faith, in order thus to benefit the Church at large, and to lead a careless world to see the reality of the things of God, by showing them in this work, that the living God is still, as 4,000 years ago, the living God. This my aim has been abundantly honoured. Multitudes of sinners have been thus converted, multitudes of the children of God in all parts of the world have been benefited by this work, even as I had anticipated. But the larger the work has grown, the greater has been the blessing, bestowed in the very way in which I looked for blessing: for the attention of hundreds of thousands has been drawn to the work; and many tens of thousands have come to see it.

All this leads me to desire further and further to labour on in this way, in order to bring yet greater glory to the Name of the Lord. *That He may be looked at, magnified, admired, trusted in,* relied on at all times, is my aim in this service; and so particularly in this intended enlargement. That it may be seen how much one poor man, simply by trusting in God, can bring about by prayer; and that thus other children of God may be led to carry on the work of God in dependence upon Him; and that children of God may be led increasingly to trust in Him in their individual positions and circumstances, therefore I am led to this further enlargement.

GEORGE MULLER (1805–1898) established a house for the care of orphans in Bristol, England, and became renowned for his practice of prayer in the support of it. He was a master of six languages, including Latin and Greek, and preached widely. He told his story in *The Autobiography of George Muller.* Biography: Basil Miller, *George Muller: Man of Faith and Miracles* (1941).

The Lifeline of Prayer
SHIRLEY DOBSON — 2002

I learned to depend on the Lord early in my childhood. During those turbulent years, my mother held our little family together. Though she wasn't a Christian at the time, she knew that she needed all the help she could get as she raised her children. So she sent my brother and me to church every Sunday, and it was there that I was introduced to Jesus Christ and invited Him into my heart.

As I learned how to pray and began speaking to the Lord, I sensed His love and care for me. Amid the chaos of our disintegrating family, this little girl found hope and comfort in Jesus. I've been praying and relying on Him ever since.

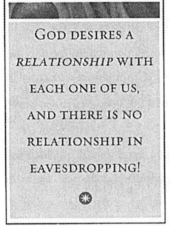

GOD DESIRES A RELATIONSHIP WITH EACH ONE OF US, AND THERE IS NO RELATIONSHIP IN EAVESDROPPING!

The many answers to prayer in my life have reinforced my belief in its power and importance. Prayer is our pathway not only to divine protection, but also to a personal, intimate relationship with God. That's why I am so honored to be in my eleventh year as chairman of the National Day of Prayer Task Force. I count it a privilege to play a small part in calling people of faith to their knees.

Jesus demonstrated the significance of this intimacy with God to His disciples. He "often withdrew to lonely places and prayed" (Luke 5:16). He "went out to a mountainside to pray, and spent the night praying to God" (Luke 6:12). He even told the disciples the parable about justice for the persistent widow "to show them that they should always pray and not give up" (Luke 18:1).

I have often wondered why the Bible places such a heavy

emphasis on prayer, especially since Jesus reminded us during the Sermon on the Mount that "your Father knows what you need before you ask him" (Matthew 6:8). When I mentioned this to my husband, his response was both simple and profound: "Well, God desires a *relationship* with each one of us, and there is no relationship in eavesdropping!"

Indeed, the Lord desires a personal, two-way conversation with me—and with you. You are His child. He wants you to seek Him, to love Him, and to spend time daily with Him. When you do, He hears and responds. Jesus said: "When you pray, go into your room, close the door and pray to your Father, who is unseen. Then your Father, who sees what is done in secret, will reward you" (Matthew 6:6).

If Christians would follow through on this truth, we would change our lives and the course of history. After all, just as prayer is important for us as individuals, it is also important to entire nations. One of my favorite Scripture verses is 2 Chronicles 7:14: "If my people, who are called by my name, will humble themselves and pray and seek my face and turn from their wicked ways, then will I hear from heaven and will forgive their sin and will heal their land."

As I reflect on this verse, I am encouraged. Prayer groups are springing up throughout America. Our nation's leaders are openly asking for prayerful support from the public. As a matter of fact, for the first time in more than a century, members of both houses of Congress met recently in the Rotunda of the

U.S. Capitol for a time of prayer and reconciliation. In the midst of our tumultuous times, God may be preparing hearts for a new openness to seeking Him through the lifeline of prayer.

SHIRLEY DOBSON has appeared on many television and radio programs with her husband, James Dobson, and serves on the board of Focus on the Family, Colorado Springs, Colorado. She has worked with Bible Study Fellowship for years, and is coauthor of *Let's Make a Memory* (with Gloria Gaither).

The Adventure of Prayer
BILL HYBELS—1988

Prayer is an unnatural activity.

From birth we have been learning the rules of self-reliance as we strain and struggle to achieve self-sufficiency. Prayer flies in the face of those deep-seated values. It is an assault on human autonomy, an indictment of independent living. To people in the fast lane, determined to make it on their own, prayer is an embarrassing interruption.

Prayer is alien to our proud human nature. And yet somewhere, someplace, probably all of us reach the point of falling to our knees, bowing our heads, fixing our attention on God and praying. We may look both ways to be sure no one is watching; we may blush; but in spite of the foreignness of the activity, we pray.

Why are we drawn to prayer? I see two possible explanations.

First, by intuition or experience we understand that *the most intimate communion with God comes only through prayer.*

Ask people who have faced tragedy or trial, heartbreak or grief, failure and defeat, loneliness or discrimination. Ask what happened in their souls when they finally fell on their knees and poured out their hearts to the Lord.

Such people have told me, "I can't explain it, but I felt like God understood me."

Others have said, "I felt surrounded by his presence."

Or, "I felt a comfort and peace I'd never felt before."

The apostle Paul knew this experience. Writing to the Christians at Philippi he said, "Do not be anxious about anything, but in everything, by prayer and petition, with thanksgiving, present your requests to God. And the peace of God, which transcends all understanding, will guard your hearts and your minds in Christ Jesus" (Phil. 4:6–7).

Several years ago my father, still a relatively young man and extremely active, died of a heart attack. As I drove to my mother's house in Michigan, I wondered how I would continue to function without the person who believed in me more than anyone else ever has or ever will.

That night in bed, I wrestled with God. "Why did this happen? How can I put it all together in my mind and in my life? Am I going to recover from losing my father? If you really love me, how could you do this to me?"

Suddenly, in the middle of the night, everything changed. It was as if I had turned a corner and was now facing a new direction. God simply said, "I'm able. I'm enough for you. Right now you doubt this, but trust me."

That experience may sound unreal, but its results were unmistakable. After that tear-filled, despairing night, I was never again tortured by doubt—either about God's care for me or about my ability to handle life without Dad. Grief, yes—his death wounded me deeply, and I will always miss him. But it did not set me adrift without anchor or compass. In the middle of the bleakest night I have ever known, one overpoweringly intimate moment with God gave me courage, reassurance and hope....

Through prayer God gives us his peace, and that is one reason even self-sufficient twentieth-century people fall on their knees and pour out their hearts to him. But there is another reason. People are drawn to prayer because they know that God's power flows primarily to people who pray.

The Scriptures are riddled with passages teaching that our almighty, omnipotent God is ready, willing and able to answer the prayers of his followers. The miracles of Israel's exodus from Egypt and journey to the Promised Land were all answers to prayer. So were Jesus' miracles of stilling storms, providing food, healing the sick and raising the dead. As the early church formed and grew and spread throughout the world, God answered the believers' continual prayers for healing and deliverance.

God's power can change circumstances and relationships. It can help us face life's daily struggles. It can heal psychological and physical problems, remove marriage obstructions, meet financial needs—in fact, it can handle any kind of difficulty, dilemma or discouragement.

Someone has said that when we work, *we* work; but when we pray, *God* works. His supernatural strength is available to praying people who are convinced to the core of their beings that he can make a difference. Skeptics may argue that answered prayers are only coincidences, but as an English archbishop once observed, "It's amazing how many coincidences occur when one begins to pray."...

When I began praying in earnest, I discovered [that God's prevailing power is released

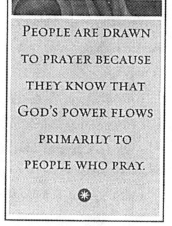

PEOPLE ARE DRAWN TO PRAYER BECAUSE THEY KNOW THAT GOD'S POWER FLOWS PRIMARILY TO PEOPLE WHO PRAY.

through prayer]. It boils down to this: if you are willing to invite God to involve himself in your daily challenges, you will experience his prevailing power—in your home, in your relationships, in the marketplace, in the schools, in the church, wherever it is most needed.

That power may come in the form of wisdom—an idea you desperately need and can't come up with yourself. It may come in the form of courage greater than you could ever muster. It may come in the form of confidence or perseverance, uncommon staying power, a changed attitude toward a spouse or a child or a parent, changed circumstances, maybe even outright miracles. However it comes, God's prevailing power is released in the lives of people who pray....

Prayerless people cut themselves off from God's prevailing power, and the frequent result is the familiar feeling of being overwhelmed, overrun, beaten down, pushed around, defeated. Surprising numbers of people are willing to settle for lives like that. Don't be one of them. Nobody has to live like that. *Prayer is the key to unlocking God's prevailing power in your life.*

> BILL HYBELS is founding pastor of the Willow Creek Community Church in South Barrington, Illinois, one of America's largest and most innovative churches. He is the author of numerous books, including *Who You Are When No One's Looking* and *Honest to God? Becoming an Authentic Christian.*

The Way of the Burning Heart
DALLAS WILLARD—1984

After his resurrection Jesus appeared to his disciples in visible form only on a very few occasions over a period of forty days. His main task as their teacher during these days was to accustom them to hearing him without seeing him. Thus it was "through the Holy Spirit" that he gave instructions to his apostles during this period (Acts 1:2). He made himself visible to them just enough to give them confidence that it was he who was speaking in their hearts. This prepared them to continue their conversation with him after he no longer appeared to them visibly.

An instructive scene from these very important days of teaching is preserved in the last chapter of Luke's Gospel. Two of Jesus' heartbroken students were walking to Emmaus, a village about seven miles northwest of Jerusalem. He caught up with them in a visible form that they did not recognize, and he heard their sad story about what had happened to Jesus of Nazareth and about how, it seemed, all hope was now lost.

He responded by taking them through the Scriptures and showing them that what had happened to their Jesus was exactly what was to befall the Messiah that Israel hoped for. Then as they sat at supper with him, suddenly "their eyes were opened, and they recognized him; and he vanished from their sight" (Lk 24:31). But their recognition was much more than a visual recognition, and that was the whole point. They asked one another, "Were not our hearts burning within us while he was talking to us on the road, while he was opening the scriptures to us?" (Lk 24:32).

What were they saying to one another? They were recalling that his words had always affected their heart, their inward life, in a peculiar way. That had been going on for about three years, and no one else had that effect on them. So they were asking themselves, "Why did we not recognize him from the way his words were impacting us?" The familiar "Jesus heartburn" had no doubt been a subject of discussion among the disciples on many occasions.

Soon he would meet with them one final time as a visible presence. There in the beauty and silence of the Galilean mountains, he would explain to them that he had been given authority over everything in heaven and on the earth. Because of that they were now to go to every kind of people on earth and make them his students, to surround them with the reality of the Father, Son and Holy Spirit and to teach them how to do all the things he had commanded.

> HE SPEAKS WITH US IN OUR HEART, WHICH BURNS FROM THE CHARACTERISTIC IMPACT OF HIS WORD. HIS PRESENCE IS TURNED INTO COMPANIONSHIP ONLY BY THE ACTUAL COMMUNICATIONS WE HAVE BETWEEN US AND HIM.
>
> ✳

You can well imagine the small degree of enthusiasm with which these poor fellows rose to greet the assignment. But his final words to them were simply, "Look, I am with you every minute, until the job is done" (Mt 28:20, paraphrase). He is with us now, and he speaks with us and we with him. He speaks with us in our heart, which burns from the characteristic impact of his word. His presence with us is, of course, much greater than his words to us. But it is turned into *companionship* only by the actual *communications* we have between us and him, communications that are frequently confirmed by external events as life moves along.

This companionship with Jesus is the form that Christian spirituality, as practiced through the ages, takes. Spiritual people are not those who engage in certain spiritual practices; they are those who *draw their life from a conversational relationship with God.* They do not live their lives merely in terms of the human order in the visible world; they have "a life beyond."

Today, as God's trusting apprentices in the kingdom of the heavens, we live on the Emmaus road, so to speak, with an intermittently burning heart. His word pours into our heart, energizing and directing our life in a way that cannot be accounted for in natural terms. The presence of the physical world is, then, if I will have it so, no longer a *barrier* between me and God. My visible surroundings become, instead, God's gift to me, where I am privileged to see the rule of heaven realized through my friendship with Jesus. He makes it so in response to my expectation. There, in some joyous measure, creation is seen moving toward "the glorious liberty of the children of God"—all because my life counts for eternity as *I* live and walk with God.

DALLAS WILLARD is professor of philosophy at the University of Southern California. His writings, especially *The Spirit of the Disciplines,* helped pioneer the recovery of the spiritual disciplines in our times. His recent writings include *The Divine Conspiracy: Rediscovering Our Hidden Life in God* and *Renovation of the Heart: Putting on the Character of Christ.*

Prayer

JAMES MONTGOMERY — *1840s*

Prayer is the soul's sincere desire,
Uttered or unexpressed,
The motion of a hidden fire
That trembles in the breast.

Prayer is the burden of a sigh,
The falling of a tear,
The upward glancing of an eye
Where none but God is near.

Prayer is the simplest form of speech
That infant lips can try;
Prayer the sublimest strains that reach
The majesty on high.

Prayer is the contrite sinner's voice
Returning from his ways,
While angels in their songs rejoice,
And cry, "Behold, he prays!"

Prayer is the Christian's vital breath,
The Christian's native air,
His watchword at the gates of death;
He enters heaven with prayer.

JAMES MONTGOMERY (1771–1854) was a Scottish poet and journalist best remembered for his hymns and versification of the Psalms (which are considered among the finest in English). The son of a Moravian minister, he published twenty-two books of verse in his lifetime. Biography: John Johansen, "James Montgomery (1771–1854): Hymn Writer and Hymnologist," *Methodist History* 10 (July 1972), 3–32.

PRAYER

Give ear to my words, O Lord,

consider my sighing.

Listen to my cry for help, my King and my God,

for to you I pray.

In the morning, O Lord, you hear my voice;

in the morning I lay my requests before you

and wait in expectation.

Psalm 5:1–3

Hear my cry, O God;

listen to my prayer.

From the ends of the earth I call to you,

I call as my heart grows faint;

lead me to the rock that is higher than I.

For you have been my refuge,

a strong tower against the foe.

Psalm 61:1–3

CHAPTER 2

THE
PSALMS
AS
PRAYER

❖

The Prayer Book of All Saints
MARTIN LUTHER—1528

[The Psalter] presents to us not the simple, ordinary speech of the saints, but the best of their language, that which they used when they talked with God himself in great earnestness and on the most important matters. Thus, the Psalter lays before us not only their words instead of their deeds, but their very hearts and the inmost treasure of the their souls, so we can look down to the foundation and source of their words and deeds. We can look into their hearts and see what kind of thoughts they had, how their hearts were disposed, and how they acted in all kinds of situations, in danger and in need....

A human heart is like a ship on a wild sea, driven by the storm winds from the four corners of the world. Here it is stuck with fear and worry about impending disaster; there comes grief and sadness because of present evil. Here breathes a

39

breeze of hope and of anticipated happiness; there blows security and joy in present blessings. These storm winds teach us to speak with earnestness, to open the heart and pour out what lies at the bottom of it....

What is the greatest thing in the Psalter but this earnest speaking amid these storm winds of every kind? Where does one find finer words of joy than in the psalms of praise and thanksgiving? There you look into the hearts of all the saints, as into fair and pleasant gardens, yes, as into heaven itself. There you see what fine and pleasant flowers of the heart spring up from all sorts of fair and happy thoughts toward God, because of his blessings. On the other hand, where do you find deeper, more sorrowful, more pitiful words of sadness than in the psalms of lamentation? There again you look into the hearts of all the saints, as into death, yes, as into hell itself....

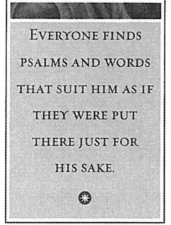

EVERYONE FINDS PSALMS AND WORDS THAT SUIT HIM AS IF THEY WERE PUT THERE JUST FOR HIS SAKE.

And that they speak these words to God and with God, this is the best thing of all. This gives the words double earnestness and life....Hence it is that the Psalter is the book of all saints; and everyone, in whatever situation he may be, finds in that situation psalms and words that fit his case, that suit him as if they were put there just for his sake, so that he could not put it better himself, or find or wish for anything better.

MARTIN LUTHER (1483–1546), a professor of Scripture at the University of Wittenberg in Germany, sparked the Protestant Reformation when he posted his "Ninety-Five Theses" in October 1517. His most influential works include *The Babylonian Captivity of the Church, The Freedom of the Christian Man,* and the first German translation of the New Testament. Biography: Roland Bainton, *Here I Stand* (1950).

How to Begin Praying
WILLIAM LAW — *1650*

There is one thing still remaining which cannot be neglected without great injury to your devotions: to begin all your prayers with a psalm.

There is nothing that so clears a way for your prayers, nothing that so disperses dullness of heart, nothing that so purifies the soul from poor and little passions, nothing that so opens heaven or carries your heart so near it as these songs of praise. They create a sense of delight in God; they awaken holy desires; they teach how to ask; and they prevail with God to give. They kindle a holy flame; they turn your heart into an altar; they turn your prayers into incense and carry them as sweet-smelling savor to the throne of grace.

WILLIAM LAW (1686–1761) was an Anglican minister, tutor, and devotional writer whose works had a profound impact upon John and Charles Wesley, George Whitfield, and other prominent leaders of the evangelical revival in eighteenth-century England. His two most famous works are *Christian Perfection* and *A Serious Call to a Devout and Holy Life*.

The Psalm As a House
WALTER WANGERIN JR. — 1998

Imagine for a moment that the psalm is like a house already built and that you are invited to enter there to make it your own. Praying from within the psalm is to pray your own prayer after all; for though you use words already written, you have become the present and living soul within those words.

Surely, some benefit shall befall you if you merely repeat the psalmist's words; but repetition is a little like walking around the outside of the house, admiring it, taking its color and shape into *your* mind, into your mouth.

The psalm desires to take you into *its* rooms. It waits to be filled with your mind and your heart. And it offers you several different doors through which you might enter and abide there.

One such door is the door of learning and analysis. As we discover the various interpretations of Hebrew words, the psalm yields its deeper meanings to us. Likewise, knowing the culture in which the psalmist wrote, the methods of worship, the views of God, the land, the conventions of Hebrew verse: all these grant us entrance into the psalm.

But there is another door which doesn't require scholarship as much as it does the keen self-awareness of the one praying. This is the door of poetry and imagination. It opens to all who knock with genuine need, so that they may go in and pray the psalm as their own....

But once you are inside the house/poem you need not be static, standing still, speaking one thought only. You may move from room to room as characters in a play move from act to act, changing as they go. Within the guidance of the psalm, *you yourself may change in the praying.* It is as if you rise several levels, from the basement to the bright air of the living room....

How does a poem work? It works *with* the reader. The reader and the poem complement each other. Like a man and a woman, they *complete* each other. The poem hints, suggests, implies—while the reader takes the hint, fills the suggestion with her own real experience, turns an implication into an open emotion and brings to life what had only lurked upon the page.

The poem invites the reader to uncover her own truth by telling her but half a truth, the other half of which is hers to find. That's the difficulty and the reward of poetry: it demands so much of the reader. It is not merely imparting information or knowledge. Rather, it wants the reader to fill its tiny frame with her *self.* But then it gives back to the reader that self, awakened and aware.

How does a psalm work? Among other things, the psalms are poems, and so they work as a poem works: *with* us, inviting us into the houses of themselves, presenting us with a part of a picture so that each one of us might imagine the rest from our own experience. Psalms shimmer into life, then, because they open themselves to *your* life.

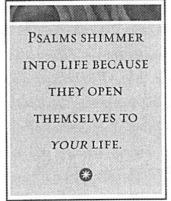

PSALMS SHIMMER INTO LIFE BECAUSE THEY OPEN THEMSELVES TO YOUR LIFE.

When you pray them this way, then, they become a special kind of poetry, the meeting place where three lives twine into one. The Psalmist, the poet, has left the hint behind him; you, the reader, by praying the psalm now breathe a present emotion into that hint; and the hint concerns the God of both, who inhabits the join between you two!

An ancient writer of the first utterance, a present voice praying, and God between: a union! The proper business of the poem-prayer.

WALTER WANGERIN JR. is writer-in-residence at Valparaiso University and the author of several award-winning books, including *The Book of the Dun Cow, The Book of God,* and *Paul: A Novel.* He lives with his wife in Valparaiso, Indiana.

An Anatomy of All Parts of the Soul
JOHN CALVIN—1540

It is hard to express in words what varied and shining riches this treasure contains: whatever I am about to say I know will fall far short of the worth of the Book of Psalms. But because it is better to give a taste, however slight, to my readers than to remain utterly silent, permit me to touch briefly on a matter whose importance cannot be completely explained. Not without reason, it is my custom to call this book *An Anatomy of All Parts of the Soul,* since there is no emotion anyone will experience whose image is not reflected in this mirror. Indeed, here the Holy Spirit has drawn to the life all pains, sorrows, fears, doubts, hopes, cares, anxieties—in short—all the turbulent emotions with which men's minds are commonly stirred.

The rest of the Scriptures contains the commandments that God enjoined upon His servants to announce to us. But here the prophets themselves speaking with God uncover all their inner feelings and call, or rather drag, each one of us to examine himself. Thus is left hidden not one of the very many infirmities to which we are subject, not one of the very many vices with which we are stuffed. A rare and singular achievement it is when, all recesses laid bare, the heart, purged of hypocrisy (most baneful infection of all), is brought into the light of day. In short, if calling upon God is the greatest bastion of our salvation, since in no other place can one seek a better and surer rule for it than in this book, it follows that, as each man best advances in understanding it, he will attain a good part of heavenly doctrine.

True prayer is born first from our own sense of need, then from faith in God's promises. Here will the readers be best awakened to sense their ills, and, as well, to seek remedies for them. Whatever can stimulate us when we are about to pray to God, this book teaches. Not only are God's promises presented to us there, but often there is shown to us someone, girding himself for prayer, caught between God's invitation and the hindrance of the flesh. Thus we are taught how, if at any time we are plagued with various doubts, to fight against them until the mind, freed, rises to God.

And not that only: but amid hesitations, fears, trepidations, we are still to rely on prayer until some solace comes. Although unfaith may shut the gate to our prayers, yet are we not to yield whenever our hearts waver or are beset with unrest, until from these struggles faith emerges victorious. In many passages we are shown God's servants so wavering in the midst of prayer that, almost overwhelmed by alternate despair and hope, they gain the prize only by hard effort.

On the one hand, the infirmity of the flesh reveals itself; on the other, the force of faith is manifested. If it is not as vigorous as might be desired, yet is it prepared to struggle until little by little it acquires perfect strength. But since the principles of proper prayer will be found scattered throughout the whole work, I shall not burden my readers with needless repetition nor hold up their progress. Only, it was worthwhile in passing to show that in this book something no less desirable is furnished to us: Not only does intimate access to God lie open to us, but infirmities that shame forbids us to confess to men, we are permitted and free to lay open before our God. Here also is precisely prescribed the proper way to offer "the sacrifice of praise," which God declares is most precious and sweet-smelling to Him. Nowhere else does one read more shining tidings of God's singular kindness to His Church and of all His works. Nowhere else are related so many deliverances, or shine so brightly proofs of his fatherly providence and care for us. Nowhere else, to sum up, is set forth a fuller reason to praise God, or are we more sharply pricked to perform this duty of piety.

JOHN CALVIN (1509–1564) of Geneva, Switzerland, was the greatest theologian of the sixteenth-century Protestant Reformation. His work *The Institutes of the Christian Religion* has been the primary shaping influence of the Reformed branch of Protestantism. Biography: T. H. L. Parker, *Portrait of Calvin.*

Learning to Pray in the Name of Jesus
DIETRICH BONHOEFFER—1940s

Now there is in the Holy Scriptures a book which is distinguished from all other books of the Bible by the fact that it contains only prayers. The book is the Psalms. It is at first very surprising that there is a prayerbook in the Bible. The Holy Scripture is the Word of God to us. But prayers are the words of men. How do prayers then get into the Bible? Let us make no mistake about it, the Bible is the Word of God even in the Psalms. Then are these prayers to God also God's own word? That seems rather difficult to understand. We grasp it only when we remember that we can learn true prayer only from Jesus Christ, from the word of the Son of God, who lives with us men, to God the Father, who lives in eternity.

Jesus Christ has brought every need, every joy, every gratitude, every hope of men before God. In his mouth the word of man becomes the Word of God, and if we pray his prayer with him, the Word of God becomes once again the word of man. All prayers of the Bible are such prayers which we pray together with Jesus Christ, in which he accompanies us, and through which he brings us into the presence of God. Otherwise there are no true prayers, for only in and with Jesus Christ can we truly pray.

If we want to read and to pray the prayers of the Bible and especially the Psalms, therefore, we must not ask first what they have to do with us, but what they have to do with Jesus Christ. We must ask how we can understand the Psalms as God's Word, and then we shall be able to pray them. It does not depend, therefore, on whether the Psalms express adequately that which we feel at a given moment in our heart. If we are to pray aright, perhaps it is quite necessary that we pray contrary to our own heart. Not what we want to pray is important, but what

God wants us to pray. If we were dependent entirely on ourselves, we would probably pray only the fourth petition of the Lord's Prayer. But God wants it otherwise. The richness of the Word of God ought to determine our prayer, not the poverty of our heart.

Thus if the Bible also contains a prayerbook, we learn from this that not only that Word which he has to say to us belongs to the Word of God, but also that word which he wants to hear from us, because it is the word of his beloved Son. This is pure grace, that God tells us how we can speak with him and have fellowship with him. We can do it by praying in the name of Jesus Christ. The Psalms are given to us to this end, that we may learn to pray them in the name of Jesus Christ.

> ALL PRAYERS OF THE BIBLE WHICH WE PRAY TOGETHER WITH JESUS CHRIST BRING US INTO THE PRESENCE OF GOD.
>
> ❂

In response to the request of the disciples, Jesus gave them the Lord's Prayer. Every prayer is contained in it. Whatever is included in the petitions of the Lord's Prayer is prayed aright; whatever is not included is no prayer. All the prayers of Holy Scripture are summarized in the Lord's Prayer, and are contained in its immeasurable breadth. They are not made superfluous by the Lord's Prayer but constitute the inexhaustible richness of the Lord's Prayer as the Lord's Prayer is their summation. Luther says of the Psalter: "It penetrates the Lord's Prayer and the Lord's

Prayer penetrates it, so that it is possible to understand one on the basis of the other and to bring them into joyful harmony." Thus the Lord's Prayer becomes the touchstone for whether we pray in the name of Jesus Christ or in our own name. It makes good sense, then, that the Psalter is often bound together in a single volume with the New Testament. It is the prayer of the Christian church. It belongs to the Lord's Prayer.

DIETRICH BONHOEFFER (1906–1945) was a Lutheran pastor, theologian, and leader of the underground Confessing Church under Hitler's regime; he was imprisoned by the Nazis and hanged shortly before the end of World War II. His most well-known works are *The Cost of Discipleship, Life Together,* and *Letters and Papers from Prison.* Biography: Eberhard Bethge, *Dietrich Bonhoeffer: A Biography.*

Praying by the Book
EUGENE H. PETERSON—*1987*

Prayer is never the first word, it is always the second word. God has the first word. Prayer is answering speech; it is not primarily "address" but "response." Essential to the practice of prayer is to fully realize this secondary quality. It is especially important in the pastoral practice of prayer since pastors are so frequently placed in positions in which it appears that our prayers have an initiating energy in them, the holy words that legitimize and bless the secular prose of committee work or community discussion or getting well or growing up....

By putting prayer in the apparent first place we contribute to its actual diminishment. By uttering a prayer to "get things started" we legitimize and bless a thin and callow secularism— everyone is now free to go his or her own way without thinking about God any more. "*That*, at least, is out of the way; now we can get to the important things that require our attention. We have pleased God with our piety and are free to get on with the things that concern *us*."...

What do we do?

We do the obvious: we restore prayer to its context in God's word....

God's word is the creative means by which everything comes into existence. The word of God constitutes the total reality in which we find ourselves. Everything we see and feel and deal with—sea and sky, codfish and warblers, sycamores and carrots—originates by means of this word. Everything, absolutely everything, was *spoken* into being... (Ps. 33:9).

This is no less true of God's parallel work, redemption. St. John, in his masterful rewriting of Genesis, wrote, "In the beginning was the Word...and the Word became flesh." The gospel spells out in detail Jesus *speaking* salvation into being: rebuking the chaos of demons, separating men and women from damnation by calling them by name into lives of discipleship, defeating the temptor with citations of Scripture, commanding healings, using words of blessing to feed and help. The *word* is as foundational in the work of salvation as it is in the work of creation....Everywhere we look, everywhere we probe, everywhere we listen we come upon *word*—and it is God's word, not ours....

Prayer is the development of speech into maturity, language in process of being adequate to answer the one who has spoken most comprehensively to us, namely, God....

Question: Where can we go to learn our language as it develops into maturity, as it answers God?

Answer: The Psalms.

The great and sprawling university that Hebrews and Christians have attended to learn to answer God, to learn to pray, has been the Psalms. More people have learned to pray by matriculating in the Psalms than any other way. The Psalms were the prayer book of Israel; they were the prayer book of Jesus; they are the prayer book of the church. At no time in the Hebrew and Christian centuries (with the possible exception of our own twentieth) have the Psalms not been at the very center of all concern and practice in prayer.

There is one large fact about the Psalms that requires notice before attending to the actual reading and praying of them— their arrangement. One hundred and fifty Psalms are arranged in five books....The five-book arrangement establishes the conditions under which we will pray, shaping a canonical context for prayer....The significance of this arrangement cannot be overstressed. It is not a minor and incidental matter of editorial tinkering; it is a major matter of orientation so that prayer will be learned properly as human *answering* speech to the *addressing* speech of God....

The Psalms provide the major documentation for what it means to answer "out of the depths" the God who addresses his people. Athanasius, the fourth-century Egyptian theologian and bishop, pointed out their unique place in the Bible: most of Scripture speaks *to* us; the Psalms speak *for* us.

The five-book arrangement of the Psalms is, then, strategic: for every word that God speaks *to* us there must be an answering word *from* us. No word of God can go unanswered. The word of God is not complete simply by being uttered; it must be answered. For the five books of God's creating/saving word to us [the Torah] there are five books of our believing/obeying word to God. Five is matched by five, like the fingers of two clasped hands.

But when we take the next step and begin to look for specific Psalm-answers to Torah-addresses we flounder. There is no apparent correspondence in subject matter between the two collections. The Torah progresses in chronological order from Adam to Moses. The Psalms are random and mixed, matching nothing specific in the Torah. Nor is there any other scheme of arrangement, such as thematic, in which various psalms are grouped together—of praise, of lament, confessions, etc. Each of the five books contains all kinds of prayers grouped together rather haphazardly....

It looks very much as if this internal nonarrangement is every bit as deliberate as the external five-book arrangement. And the reason is not far to seek: there are no stock catechism answers here for the simple reason that that is not the way communication takes place between living persons. The life that God calls into being in us is enormously various and infinitely complex. Rote responses are not adequate to the dazzling creativity of address that is put to us by God's word. What is required in us is not that we learn a specific answer to a specific address, but that we acquire facility in personal language that is accurately responsive to what we hear God say to us out of his word in Scripture and in Christ in our changing situations and various levels of faith....

So Psalm 1 is not the stock prayer-answer to Genesis 1, nor Psalm 2 to Genesis 2. What Psalm 1 does is introduce us to words and rhythms that will provide us with the means to answer Exodus 16 on one day and Deuteronomy 4 on another. I read Numbers 22 one way when I was a seventeen-year-old student, another way as a forty-five-year-old pastor, and accurately both times. But my answers were accurate only when they spoke an obedience and faith issuing from a thoroughly personal and physical actual present. I need a language that is large enough to maintain continuities and supple enough to express nuances across a lifetime that brackets child and adult experiences, and courageous enough to explore all the countries of sin and salvation, mercy and grace, creation and covenant, anxiety and trust, unbelief and faith that comprise the continental human condition. The Psalms are this large, supple, and courageous language. John Calvin called the 150 Psalms an "anatomy of all the parts of the soul." Everything that a person can possibly feel, experience, and say is brought into expression before God in the Psalms.

If we insist on being self-taught in prayer, our prayers, however eloquent, will be meagre. Inevitably they will be shaped on the one hand by whatever the congregational "market" demands, and restricted by our own little faith on the other....It is no easy thing, venturing out of our cozy small-minded religious programs into a large-souled obedience, leaving the secure successes of our professionally defined lives and living by faith and love in prayer (which frequently involves failure and suffering). Where will we acquire a language that is adequate for these intensities? Where else but in the Psalms?

For men and women...of faith, apprenticeship in the Psalms is not an option; it is a mandate....Prayer must not be fabricated out of emotional fragments or professional duties. Uninstructed and untrained, our prayers are something learned by tourists out of a foreign language phrase book: we give thanks at meals, repent of the grosser sins, bless the Rotary picnic, and ask for occasional guidance. Did we think prayer was merely a specialized and incidental language to get by on during those moments when we happened to pass through a few miles of religious country? But our entire lives are involved. We need fluency in the language of the country we live in....

Praying the Psalms, we find the fragments of our soul and body, our own and all those with whom we have to do, spoken into adoration and love and faith....St. Ambrose called the Psalms "a sort of gymnasium for the use of all souls, a sort of stadium of virtue, where different sorts of exercise are set out before him, from which he can choose the best suited to train him to win his crown."

EUGENE H. PETERSON is the translator of the widely acclaimed translation of the Bible, *The Message,* and the author of numerous books, including *A Long Obedience in the Same Direction, Answering God,* and *Reversed Thunder.* He was a pastor for many years and, later, professor of spiritual theology at Regent College.

Praying in the Rawness of Life
WALTER BRUEGGEMANN—*1982*

I suggest, in a simple schematic fashion, that our life of faith consists in moving with God in...(a) being securely *oriented,* (b) being painfully *disoriented,* and (c) being surprisingly *reoriented.* This general way of speaking can apply to our *self*-acceptance, our relations to significant *others,* our participation in *public issues.* It can permit us to speak of "passages," the life-cycle, stages of growth, and identity crises. It can permit us to be honest about what is happening to us. Most of all, it may provide us a way to think about the Psalms in relation to our common human experience, for each of God's children is in transit along the flow of orientation, disorientation, and reorientation.

The first situation in this scheme, that of being securely oriented, is a situation of equilibrium. While we all yearn for it, it is not very interesting and it does not produce great prayer or powerful song. It consists in being well-settled, knowing that life makes sense and God is well placed in heaven, presiding but not bothering. This is the mood of much of the middle-class Church....This mood...is minimal in the Psalms but may be reflected in Ps. 37;...and it is more eloquently reflected in such a marvelous statement as Ps. 145, which trusts everything to God. Such Psalms reflect confident well-being. In order to pray them, we must locate either in our lives or in the lives of others situations of such confident, buoyant, "successful" living.

> THINK ABOUT THE PSALMS IN RELATION TO OUR COMMON HUMAN EXPERIENCE, FOR EACH OF GOD'S CHILDREN IS IN TRANSIT ALONG THE FLOW OF ORIENTATION, DISORIENTATION, AND REORIENTATION.

But that is a minor theme in the Psalms and not very provocative. The Psalms mostly do not emerge out of such situations of equilibrium. Rather, people are driven to such poignant prayer and song as are found in the Psalter precisely by *experiences of dislocation and relocation.* It is experiences of being overwhelmed, nearly destroyed, and surprisingly given life which empower us to pray and sing....

The events at the edge of our humanness, i.e., the ones that threaten and disrupt our convenient equilibrium, are the events which may fill us with passion and evoke in us eloquence....As we enter into the prayer and song of common humanity in the Psalms, it is helpful to be attentive precisely to the simple eloquence, the overriding passion, and the bold ways in which this voice turns to the Holy One....

The Psalms...propose to speak about human experience in an honest, freeing way. This is in contrast to much human speech and conduct which is in fact a cover-up. In most arenas where people live, we are expected and required to speak the language of safe orientation and equilibrium, either to find it so or to pretend we find it so. For the normal, conventional functioning of public life, the raw edges of disorientation and reorientation must be denied or suppressed for purposes of public equilibrium. As a result, our speech is dulled and mundane. Our passion has been stilled and is without imagination. And mostly the Holy One is not addressed, not because we dare not, but because God is far away and hardly seems important. This means that the agenda and intention of the Psalms is considerably at odds with the normal speech of most people, the normal speech of a stable, functioning, self-deceptive culture in which everything must be kept running young and smooth.

Against that, the speech of the Psalms is abrasive, revolutionary, and dangerous. It announces that life is not like that, that our common experience is not one of well-being and equilibrium, but a churning, disruptive experience of dislocation and relocation. Perhaps in our conventional, routinized prayer life...that is one of the reasons the Psalter does not yield its power—because out of habit or fatigue or numbness, we try to use the Psalms in our equilibrium. And when we do that, we miss the point of the Psalms....

Thus I suggest that most of the Psalms can only be appropriately prayed by people who are living at the edge of their lives, sensitive to the raw hurts, the primitive passions, and the naïve elations that are at the bottom of our life. For most of us, liturgical or devotional entry into the Psalms requires a real change of pace. It asks us to depart from the closely managed world of public survival, to move into the open, frightening, healing world of speech with the Holy One.

WALTER BRUEGGEMANN is professor of Old Testament at Columbia Theological Seminary and the author of many books on the Bible, including *Spirituality of the Psalms, Israel's Praise, The Bible Makes Sense,* and *A Commentary on Jeremiah.*

Lament

James Houston — *1996*

When life is going well for us, we can become soulless and complacent before God, putting ourselves out of touch of his mercy. God may put us through periods of intense emotional and moral disorientation, during which we can do nothing except lament before him.

The book of Psalms is full of such prayers. These songs of lament and confession are characterized by certain recurring features.

The writer begins with a plea that God will correct his desperate situation. He addresses God personally, declaring that he trusts God despite great distress, or even intense anger.

A long complaint at the desperate situation then follows. This could be a case of prolonged illness, an agonized conscience, isolation, imprisonment, or the destruction of life. God is accused of allowing these things to happen.

The writer now asks God to act quickly and decisively. He uses strong language to plead for justice, or mercy, suggesting that if God had been more attentive, then these things might never have happened!

Having vented his feelings so strongly, the writer can now recognize some of God's true motives, which he was unable to see before. He begins to achieve a better perspective on his troubles. A few self-doubts creep in. Perhaps he was wrong in the way he accused God. Anger and cursing may still linger as an echo of the bitterness and resentment within. The writer's old way of life has not been completely changed.

Once he has received healing and forgiveness, the writer can praise God with the assurance that his prayer has been heard. He promises to serve God in a renewed life, full of praise and worship.

This type of prayer is an act of cleansing. It purges sin, dissolves misunderstanding about God, removes doubt about God's actions, and washes out all the deceitfulness that sin has created within us. Confession is therefore a great antidote to the poison of mistrust in our lives. Such honest exposure of our condition before God shows up any secret, lurking distrust within us. It helps to weaken addictive, sinful habits....

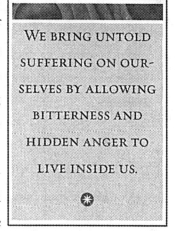

WE BRING UNTOLD SUFFERING ON OUR-SELVES BY ALLOWING BITTERNESS AND HIDDEN ANGER TO LIVE INSIDE US.

There is a vast realm of stress-related illness in our society and within ourselves, caused when we repress our anxiety and guilt. If prayer helps us to counteract selfish living, it also provides us with the release of suppressed emotions. We bring untold suffering on ourselves by allowing bitterness, hidden anger, and so many other negative emotions to live inside us....

As we open the depths of our lives to God, we will grow in the use of prayer that cries out to God for help. Many Christians have discovered from their own experience that short prayers for help are more effective than long, exhaustive prayers. A simple prayer from the Psalms, such as "Create in me a clean heart, O God, and renew a right spirit within me," repeated throughout the day, can help us to find the attitude we need to take before God. The Psalms are full of these short prayers, and we can ransack the book to find the ones which best meet our needs.

JAMES HOUSTON was the founding principal and chancellor of Regent College in Vancouver, British Columbia, and has served as professor of spiritual theology there. He is also the author of *The Heart's Desire* and *In Pursuit of Happiness.*

Christ's Last Prayer
AMY CARMICHAEL — 1930s

Do you ever find prayer difficult because of tiredness or dryness? When that is so, it is an immense help to let the psalms and hymns we know by heart say themselves or sing themselves inside us. This is possible anywhere and at any time.

We can't be mistaken in using this easy, open way of prayer, for our Lord Jesus used it. His very last prayer, when He was far too tired to pray as He usually did, was Psalm 31:5, "Into

Thine hand I commit my spirit: Thou has redeemed me, O Lord God of truth." Every Jewish mother used to teach her child to say those words as a good-night prayer.

Hymns, little prayer-songs of our own, even the simplest of them, can sing us into His love. Or more truly, into the consciousness of His love, for we are never for one moment out of it.

AMY CARMICHAEL (1867–1951) served as a missionary in South India from 1895 until her death in 1951. In 1931 she was stricken with a confining illness for the remaining years of her life, but she continued to counsel people and write many books, including *Candle in the Dark, Gold by Moonlight,* and *Edges of His Ways.* Biography: Elizabeth Skoglund, *Amma: The Life and Words of Amy Carmichael* (1994).

Finding Timely Words
ANTHONY BLOOM — *1970*

There is a need for some sort of prayer which is not spontaneous but which is truly rooted in conviction. To find this you can draw from a great many of the existing prayers. We already have a rich panoply of prayers which were wrought in the throes of faith, by the Holy Spirit. For example, we have the Psalms, we have so many short and long prayers in the liturgical wealth of all the Churches from which we can draw. What matters is that you should learn and know enough of such prayers so that at the right moment you are able to find the right prayers. It is a question of learning by heart enough meaningful passages, from the Psalms or from the prayers of the saints.

Each of us is sensitive to certain particular passages. Mark these passages that go deep into your heart, that move you deeply, that make sense, that express something which is already within your experience, either of sin, or of bliss in God, or of struggle. Learn those passages, because one day when you are so completely low, so profoundly desperate that you cannot call out of your soul any spontaneous expression, any spontaneous wording, you will discover that these words come up and offer themselves to you as a gift of God, as a gift of the Church, as a gift of holiness, helping our simple lack of strength. And then you really need the prayers you have learnt and made a part of yourself.

ANTHONY BLOOM has served, since 1962, as Archbishop of the Russian Orthodox Patriarchal Church in Great Britain and Ireland. He was trained as a physician and worked as a surgeon in Paris during World War II. His books on prayer are widely read around the world, especially *Creative Prayer, Living Prayer,* and *Courage to Pray.*

PRAYER

This, then, is how you should pray:
"Our Father in heaven,
hallowed be your name,
your kingdom come,
your will be done on earth as it is in heaven.
Give us today our daily bread.
Forgive us our debts,
as we also have forgiven our debtors.
And lead us not into temptation,
but deliver us from the evil one."

MATTHEW 6:9–13

CHAPTER 3

PATTERNS
FOR
PRAYER

❋

Two Simple Ways of Praying
JEANNE GUYON—*1710*

I would like to address you as though you were a beginner in Christ, one seeking to know Him. In so doing, let me suggest two ways for you to come to the Lord. I will call the first way "praying the Scripture;" the second way I will call "beholding the Lord" or "waiting in His presence."

"Praying the Scripture" is a unique way of dealing with the Scripture; it involves both reading and prayer. Here is how you should begin.

Turn to the Scripture; choose some passage that is simple and fairly practical. Next, come to the Lord. Come quietly and humbly. There, before Him, read a small portion of the passage of Scripture you have opened to. Be careful as you read. Take in fully, gently and carefully what you are reading. Taste it and digest it as you read.

In the past it may have been your habit, while reading, to move very quickly from one verse of Scripture to another until you had read the whole passage. Perhaps you were seeking to find the main point of the passage.

But in coming to the Lord by means of "praying the Scripture," you do not read quickly; you read very slowly. You do not move from one passage to another, not until you have

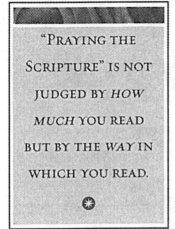

"PRAYING THE SCRIPTURE" IS NOT JUDGED BY *HOW MUCH* YOU READ BUT BY THE *WAY* IN WHICH YOU READ.

sensed the very heart of what you have read. You may then want to take that portion of Scripture that has touched you and turn it into prayer.

After you have sensed something of the passage and after you know that the essence of that portion has been extracted and all the deeper sense of it is gone, then, very slowly, gently, and in a calm manner begin to read the next portion of the passage. You will be surprised to find that when your time with the Lord has ended, you will have read very little, probably no more than half a page.

"Praying the Scripture" is not judged by *how much* you read but by the *way* in which you read.

If you read quickly, it will benefit you little. You will be like a bee that merely skims the surface of a flower. Instead, in this new way of reading with prayer, you must become as the bee who penetrates into the *depths* of the flower. You plunge deeply within to remove its deepest nectar.

Of course, there is a kind of reading the Scripture for scholarship and for study—but not here. That studious kind of reading will not help you when it comes to matters that are *divine!* To receive any deep, inward profit from the Scripture, you must read as I have described. Plunge into the very depths of the words you read until revelation, like a sweet aroma, breaks out upon you.

I am quite sure that if you will follow this course, little by little you will come to experience a very rich prayer that flows from your inward being....

The second kind of prayer, which I described as "beholding the Lord" or "waiting on the Lord," *also* makes use of the Scripture but is not actually a time of reading.

Remember, I am addressing you as if you were a new convert. Here is your second way to encounter Christ. And this second way to Christ, although you will be using the Scripture, has a purpose altogether different from "praying the Scripture." For that reason you should set aside a separate time when you can come just to wait upon Him.

In "praying the Scripture" you are seeking to find the Lord in what you are reading, in the very words themselves. In this path, therefore, the content of the Scripture is the focal point of your attention. Your purpose is to take everything from the passage that unveils the Lord to you.

What of this second path? In "beholding the Lord," you come to the Lord in a totally different way. Perhaps at this point I need to share with you the greatest difficulty you will have in waiting upon the Lord. It has to do with your mind. The mind has a very strong tendency to stray away from the Lord. Therefore, as you come before your Lord to sit in His presence, beholding Him, make use of the Scripture *to quiet your mind*. The way to do this is really quite simple.

First, read a passage of Scripture. Once you sense the Lord's presence, the content of what you have read is no longer important. The Scripture has served its purpose; it has quieted your mind; it has brought you to Him.

So that you can see this more clearly, let me describe the way in which you come to the Lord by the simple act of beholding Him and waiting upon Him.

You begin by setting aside a time to be with the Lord. When you do come to Him, come quietly. Turn your heart to the presence of God. How is this done? This, too, is quite simple. You turn to Him by *faith*. By faith you believe you have come into the presence of God.

Next, while you are before the Lord, begin to read some portion of Scripture. As you read, *pause*. The pause should be quite gentle. You have paused so that you may set your mind on the Spirit. You have set your mind *inwardly*—on Christ....

While you are before the Lord, hold your heart in His presence. How? This you also do by faith. Yes, by faith you can hold your heart in the Lord's presence. Now, waiting before Him, turn all your attention toward your spirit. Do not allow your mind to wander. If your mind begins to wander, just turn your attention back again to the inward parts of your being.

You will be free from wandering—free from any outward distractions—and you will be brought near to God.…

Once your heart has been turned inwardly to the Lord, you will have an impression of His presence. You will be able to notice His presence more acutely because your outer senses have now become very calm and quiet. Your attention is no longer on outward things or on the surface thoughts of your mind; instead, sweetly and silently, your mind becomes occupied with what you have read and by that touch of His presence.

Oh, it is not that you will think about what you have read, but you will *feed* upon what you have read. Out of a love for the Lord you exert your will to hold your mind quiet before Him. When you have come to this state, you must allow your mind to rest.

How shall I describe what to do next?

In this very peaceful state, *swallow* what you have tasted. At first this may seem difficult, but perhaps I can show you just how simple it is. Have you not, at times, enjoyed the flavor of a very tasty food? But unless you were willing to swallow the food, you received no nourishment. It is the same with your soul. In this quiet, peaceful, and simple state, simply take in what is there as nourishment.

JEANNE GUYON (1648–1717) was a French Christian mystic and writer who was arrested and imprisoned several times and whose writings were condemned by the French Church. Her most important work was *The Short and Very Easy Method of Prayer* (1685). Biography: Dorothy Coslet, *Madame Jeanne Guyon* (1998).

Luther's Way to Pray
MARTIN LUTHER—1535

Dear Master Peter:

I will tell you as best I can what I do personally when I pray. May our dear Lord grant to you and to everybody to do it better than I! Amen.

First, when I feel that I have become cool and joyless in prayer because of other tasks or thoughts (for the flesh and the devil always impede and obstruct prayer), I take my little psalter, hurry to my room, or, if it be the day and hour for it, to the church where a congregation is assembled and, as time permits, I say quietly to myself and word-for-word the Ten Commandments, the Creed, and, if I have time, some words of Christ or Paul, or some psalms, just as a child might do.

It is a good thing to let prayer be the first business of the morning and the last at night. Guard yourself carefully against those false, deluding ideas which tell you, "Wait a little while. I will pray in an hour; first I must attend to this or that." Such thoughts get you away from prayer into other affairs which so hold your attention and involve you that nothing comes of prayer for that day....

We must be careful not to break the habit of true prayer and imagine other works to be necessary which, after all, are nothing of the kind. Thus at the end we become lax and lazy, cool and listless toward prayer. The devil who besets us is not lazy or careless, and our flesh is too ready and eager to sin and is disinclined to the spirit of prayer.

When your heart has been warmed by such recitation to yourself [of the Ten Commandments, the words of Christ, etc.] and is intent upon the matter, kneel or stand with your hands folded and your eyes toward heaven and speak or think as briefly as you can:

O Heavenly Father, dear God, I am a poor unworthy sinner. I do not deserve to raise my eyes or hands toward thee or to pray. But because thou hast commanded us all to pray and hast promised to hear us and through thy dear Son Jesus Christ hast taught us both how and what to pray, I come to thee in obedience to thy word, trusting in thy gracious promise. I pray in the name of my Lord Jesus Christ together with all thy saints and Christians on earth as he has taught us: Our Father who art, etc., through the whole prayer, word for word.

Then repeat one part or as much as you wish, perhaps the first petition: "Hallowed be thy name."...

Finally, mark this, that you must always speak the Amen firmly. Never doubt that God in his mercy will surely hear you and say "yes" to your prayers. Never think that you are kneeling or standing alone, rather think that the whole of Christendom, all devout Christians, are standing there beside you and you are standing among them in common, united petition which God cannot disdain. Do not leave your prayer without having said or thought, "Very well, God has heard my prayer; this I know as a certainty and a truth." That is what Amen means.

You should also know that I do not want you to recite all these words in your prayer. That would make it nothing but idle chatter and prattle, read word for word out of a book as

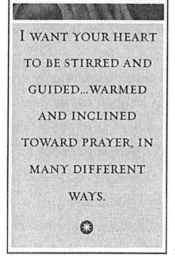

I WANT YOUR HEART TO BE STIRRED AND GUIDED...WARMED AND INCLINED TOWARD PRAYER, IN MANY DIFFERENT WAYS.

were the rosaries by the laity and the prayers of the priests and monks. Rather do I want your heart to be stirred and guided concerning the thoughts which ought to be comprehended in the Lord's Prayer. These thoughts may be expressed, if your heart is rightly warmed and inclined toward prayer, in many different ways and with more words or fewer. I do not bind myself to such words or syllables, but say my prayers in one fashion today, in another tomorrow, depending upon my mood and feeling. I stay however, as nearly as I can, with the same general thoughts and ideas.

It may happen occasionally that I may get lost among so

many ideas in one petition that I forego the other six. If such an abundance of good thoughts comes to us we ought to disregard the other petitions, make room for such thoughts, listen in silence, and under no circumstances obstruct them. The Holy Spirit himself preaches here, and one word of his sermon is far better than a thousand of our prayers. Many times I have learned more from one prayer than I might have learned from much reading and speculation.

For biographical information on this author, see page 41.

Four Basic Steps to Conversational Prayer
ROSALIND RINKER — 1966

The purpose of these four steps to prayer is to give beginners in prayer a place to start—a workable plan. They will serve as a pattern-breaker to replace previous attempts which ended either in failure or cold conformity. You will find the painful self-consciousness slipping away unnoticed as you begin to concentrate on the meaning of these four steps....

1. Jesus is here. Matthew 18:19–20
2. Thank You, Lord. Philippians 4:4–7
3. Help me, Lord. James 5:13–16
4. Help my brother. Mark 11:22–25

Read them again. There are only three words in each step. Look away from the page now, and repeat them. You will never forget them, and you will find yourself following them at the most unlikely moment—which is the way prayer ought to be offered.

All you may have learned in your own private school of prayer can be fitted into these steps, and once you've used them, you'll find the order is not important. I am not trying to teach you a method. I am attempting to teach you to speak with a Person who loves you. These guide lines are intended to quickly and easily make the "how-to" part both familiar and workable....

1. *Jesus is here.*

There is no problem praying when God is near. To feel His nearness, you act on the knowledge of the truth of His presence. You will increasingly learn how to make use of your creative imagination. The Spirit of Christ will be there with you, whether or not you feel Him.

(For the leader: This is a time for silent worship, with participants centering on the thoughts you give them. Read Matthew 18:19–20. A suggested opening is: "Hear the words of Jesus… (read the verses). Let us forget one another and remember we want to be as little children at the feet of Jesus." You may use other ideas or Scripture, but keep the meditation very short, very specific, suggesting *Christ with us,* here and now.)

2. *Thank You, Lord.*

The first step is the beginning of silent worship together. The second step is a continuation of worship in which all participate. Giving thanks is a form of worship which opens not only mouths, but hearts. Let your sentence prayers be brief. If you have two "thank you's" then pray twice, letting others pray too.

(For leaders: These first steps are a unit of worship in receiving love. The next two are a unit in giving love. You may have to remind them several times to give thanks for only *one* thing at a time. This, in the beginning, encourages many to take part who otherwise might remain silent.)

3. *Help me, Lord.*

At this time (God will guide you) you must decide whether or not you wish to admit a specific fault or need. If you do, those present will pray for you.

(For leaders: You will need wisdom and discernment when you introduce this third step. Much will depend upon those present. Sometimes the group needs to be broken into twos or threes for periods of five or ten minutes. If this third step is consistently omitted, a lack of personal honesty and healing love is fostered, and the result is a rather "cold" prayer time.)

4. *Help my brother.*

As soon as a person prays for himself, another one or two should be applying a "band-aid" of love upon that wounded spirit. Any revealing of the heart calls for immediate response on the part of those who heard the prayer. Let your prayer-response be brief, to the point, with thanksgiving and with love. And without preaching or suggesting! Prayer should involve neither of these. We pray for each other by name, back and forth sometimes, according to the discernment received through listening and through loving. It is important that the group be small so first names—yes, first names—of those present are used. Prayer then becomes a more meaningful act of personal love and concern....

We are simply outlining a fresh approach to loving one another as Christ has loved us, by praying together. We can consciously receive His love when we are consciously in His presence; then we have an abundant supply to give away. To learn to give love and care through praying together results in sudden joy springing up in all our hearts....

Do people who are unable to pray become reborn when they pray? Yes, they do. I found when I explain these four steps and announce a demonstration of them, people are eager to learn. I invite those desiring to participate to meet me after the lecture in a certain place. For five or ten minutes we stand together in a circle as I lead them into an actual experience of conversational prayer by following the four basic steps.

Do you wish to discover joy in prayer?

Open your heart willingly for Jesus to love you.

Follow these four basic steps.

And start praying now with one other person. If you don't know who that will be, ask God—He'll show you.

ROSALIND RINKER (1907–2002) served as a missionary with the Oriental Missionary Society and a counselor and staff member with InterVarsity Christian Fellowship. She is the author of many books on prayer, including *Prayer: Conversing with God* and *How to Get the Most out of Your Prayer Life.*

The Jesus Prayer

ANTHONY CONIARIS — 1982

The prayer in which the spiritual tradition of the Eastern Church finds its deepest expression is the Jesus Prayer consisting of the simple words: "Lord Jesus Christ, Son of God, have mercy on me."

In the book *The Way of a Pilgrim* a Russian peasant tells how he traveled from village to village, and monastery to monastery trying to find someone to teach him how to pray unceasingly (I Thess. 5:17). Finally he finds a monk who teaches him the Jesus Prayer by reading to him the following words of St. Symeon the New Theologian: "Sit down alone and in silence. Lower your head, shut your eyes, breathe out gently and imagine yourself looking into your own heart. Carry your mind, i.e., your thoughts, from your head to your heart. As you breathe out say: 'Lord Jesus, have mercy on me.' Say it moving your lips gently, or say it in your mind. Try to put all other thoughts aside. Be calm, be patient and repeat the process very frequently."

After following these instructions and reaching the point where he could repeat this prayer thousands of times a day, the pilgrim says:

"Under this guidance I spent the whole summer in ceaseless

oral prayer to Jesus Christ, and I felt absolute peace in my soul. During sleep I often dreamed I was saying the Prayer. And during the day, if I happened to meet anyone, all men without exception were as dear to me as if they had been my nearest relations...I thought of nothing whatever but my Prayer, my mind tended to listen to it, and my heart began of itself to feel at times a certain warmth and pleasure."

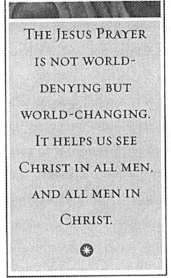

THE JESUS PRAYER IS NOT WORLD-DENYING BUT WORLD-CHANGING. IT HELPS US SEE CHRIST IN ALL MEN, AND ALL MEN IN CHRIST.

The Jesus Prayer transforms the pilgrim's relationship with the material creation about him, changing all things into icons or sacraments of God's presence. He writes:

"When I prayed with my heart, everything around me seemed delightful and marvelous. The trees, the grass, the birds, the earth, the air, the light seemed to be telling me that they existed for man's sake, that they witnessed to the love of God for man, that everything proved the love of God for man, that all things prayed to God and sang His praise. Thus it was that I came to understand what 'The Philokalia' calls 'the knowledge of the speech of all creatures'...I felt a burning love for Jesus Christ and for all God's creatures."

The Jesus Prayer transfigured the pilgrim's relation not only with the material world but also with other people. He writes:

"Again I started off on my wanderings. But now I did not walk alone as before, filled with care. The Invocation of the Name of Jesus gladdened my way. Everybody was kind to me, it was as though everyone loved me...If anyone harms me I have only to think, 'How sweet is the Prayer of Jesus!' and the injury and the anger alike pass away and I forget it all."

From these words we see that the Jesus Prayer is not world-denying but world-changing. It helps us see Christ in all men, and all men in Christ....

St. Nicodemos the Hagiorite writes on the function of the Jesus Prayer in our salvation: "Because, brethren, we have fallen into sins after baptism and consequently have buried the grace of the Holy Spirit which was given to us at our Baptism, it is necessary that we make every effort to recover that original grace which is found deeply buried underneath our passions, like an ember in the ashes. This ember of grace we must fan into a new flame in our hearts. In order to do that, we must remove the passions from our hearts as ashes from a fireplace, and replace them with the firewood of obedience in the life-giving commandments of the Lord. We can blow upon the spark with heartfelt repentance of the mind and with the repetition of this prayer: 'Lord Jesus Christ, Son and Word of God, have mercy on me.' When this prayer remains permanently in our heart, it cleanses us...with a wondrous and strange fire. The fire, on the one hand, burns away the temptation of evil thoughts, and on the other, it sweetens the whole inner person and enlightens the mind."

The division of prayer into three parts—of the body (lips), of the mind, and of the heart—applies also to the Jesus Prayer. It begins as a prayer of the lips and the tongue that is prayed orally. Gradually it becomes more inward and is prayed silently with the mind. It becomes "a small murmuring stream" within. Finally, it enters the heart and dominates the entire personality. Then we have received the gift of unceasing prayer. The Jesus Prayer continues uninterrupted within us even when we are engaged in other activities....

And so we pray: "Lord Jesus Christ, Son of God, have mercy on me a sinner."

ANTHONY CONIARIS is pastor emeritus of St. Mary's Orthodox Church and president of Light and Life Publishing Company in Minneapolis, Minnesota. He is the author of *Discovering God Through the Daily Practice of His Presence, Introducing the Orthodox Church,* and many other books.

Holy Reading
MARTIN L. SMITH — *1989*

"Taste and see that the Lord is good" (Ps. 34:8)....

There is a very ancient form of meditation on Scripture for which tasting and eating and digesting is the most obvious metaphor. It stems from the way our predecessors read and was especially cultivated in the monasteries. Its old title in Latin is "lectio divina," which means holy reading. This way of prayer consists in reading very slowly through a passage until a particular word or phrase "lights up" and attracts the reader. The text is then laid aside and the phrase is repeated in the heart. The one praying simply repeats the phrase, allowing it to unfold without any analysis. When the phrase has been deeply absorbed, it is time for responding to God by expressing the feelings the words have evoked, the needs, desires, the appreciation or praise, in the simplest possible way. If words seem to sink away, then the prayer consists in staying still in the awareness the meditation has fostered, being in and with God. Then when distractions bring this state of awareness to an end the meditation is brought to a conclusion or, if more time is available, the reading can be gently resumed....

Here is a set of guidelines for holy reading. At first it is advisable to pray with texts you have at least some familiarity with. If you try holy reading with a part of Scripture that is completely strange to you, your curiosity may be aroused and it will be very tempting to race ahead to see what comes next. The meditation is not intended to introduce you to something new. It is meant to allow you to *experience* and feed on what you know. Regular reading of the Bible extends the *breadth* of our familiarity with Scripture. In "holy reading" we absorb the Word in *depth*.

1. Spend a few minutes settling down and pray that your heart may be opened and receptive to the gift God knows you

need today. Only the Breath, the Spirit of God, can bring the word to life. Let your own breathing become more deep-seated, gentler, from lower down, as you invite the Spirit to pray in you afresh.

2. Begin reading at the place you have previously chosen, and read on very slowly indeed with an open mind. Don't study the text, just read it slowly, aloud if you find that helpful. This is the "lectio," or reading.

3. When a particular sentence or phrase or single word "lights up" or "rings a bell," seems striking or inviting, put the Bible down. Resist the temptation to go on, and do not start thinking up reasons why the phrase has claimed your attention. Here the reading stops and the "meditatio" begins, the absorption through repetition. So, for example, you might be reading the tenth chapter of John's gospel where Jesus describes himself as the Good Shepherd. As you come to verse 14 these words seem to have a special allure, "I know my own, and my own know me." This is the verse you now meditate with.

4. Gently repeat this phrase or word again and again within the heart. Don't project them outward. Let the repetition be gentle and not mechanical. There is no need to conjure up any mental picture to accompany the words or to try to make yourself feel any particular emotion as you speak them. Resist the temptation to force particular lessons or meanings from the words....In time you will become aware of an impression that

84

the words have made on you. They have evoked a particular feeling or attitude. When you have become aware of this there is no need to prolong the repetition. Now is the time for "oratio," the praying of your response.

5. Express to God in the simplest way the impression the words have made on you. You may want to thank God for the gift they convey, ask the questions they have stirred in you, put into words the longings or needs they have brought up. Keep it simple, praying spontaneously....Your prayer may move into contemplation, a simple being in Christ with God in which all you are aware of is that you are being attracted towards God like the needle of a compass finding the north.

6. After some time you will not be able to sustain your spontaneous praying or state of loving awareness. Distractions set in. You may bring the prayer time to a close with thanksgiving or by reciting the Lord's Prayer. If you have time and opportunity, you may feel drawn to begin the process again by returning to the Scripture. Begin at the point where you left off and continue with the reading expecting to be touched again by another word.

MARTIN L. SMITH is an Episcopal priest and a member of the Society of Saint John the Evangelist in Cambridge, Massachusetts. He is a spiritual director, preacher, retreat leader, and the author of a number of books on prayer and the spiritual life, including *Co-Creators with God* and *Love Set Free.*

A Pattern for Prayer

BILL HYBELS—1988

Developing prayer fitness is like developing physical fitness: you need a pattern to avoid becoming imbalanced. Without a routine, you will probably fall into the "Please God" trap: "Please God, give me. Please God, help me. Please God, cover me. Please God, arrange this."

Oh, occasionally you'll toss a few thanks heavenward when you notice that God has allowed some good thing to come your way. Every once in a while, if you get caught with your hand in the cookie jar, you'll confess a momentary lapse of sound judgment. And now and then, if you're feeling really spiritual, you might even throw a little worship into your prayers—but only as the Spirit leads.

If I sound sarcastic, it's because I know all about imbalanced prayer—I'm a real pro in that department. And I can tell you from personal experience where imbalanced prayer leads. Sensing the carelessness and one-sidedness of your prayers, you begin to feel guilty about praying. Guilt leads to faint-heartedness, and that in turn leads to prayerlessness. When praying makes you feel guilty, pretty soon you stop praying.

If that has happened to you, it's time to set up a prayer routine.

I'm going to offer you a pattern to follow. It's not the only pattern or the perfect pattern, but it's a good pattern that has been used for many years in Christian circles. It's balanced, and it's easy to use. All you have to remember is the word ACTS, an acrostic whose four letters stand for *adoration, confession, thanksgiving* and *supplication.*

Start with Adoration

In my opinion, it is absolutely essential to begin times of prayer with adoration, or worship....*First, adoration sets the tone for the entire prayer.* It reminds us whom we are addressing, whose presence we have entered, whose attention we have gained. How often our problems and trials and needs seem so pressing that we reduce prayer to a wish list! But when we commit ourselves to beginning all our prayers with adoration, we have to slow down and focus our attention on God....

Second, adoration reminds us of God's identity and inclination. As we list his attributes, lifting up his character and personality, we reinforce our understanding of who he is....

You can praise God for being faithful, righteous, just, merciful, gracious, willing to provide, attentive, unchanging. When in a spirit of adoration you begin going through God's attributes, you will soon say from the heart, "I am praying to a tremendous God!" And that motivates you to continue praying.

Third, adoration purifies the one who is praying. When you have spent a few minutes praising God for who he is, your spirit is softened and your agenda changes. Those burning issues you were dying to bring to God's attention may seem less crucial. Your sense of desperation subsides as you focus on

God's greatness, and you can truly say, "I am enjoying you, God; it is well with my soul." Adoration purges your spirit and prepares you to listen to God....

Pick out a psalm of praise and read or say it to him. Some of the best known are Psalms 8, 19, 23, 46, 95, 100, and 148; but go through the whole book and see what you can find. Two other wonderful psalms of praise are the Magnificat (Lk 1:46–55) and Zechariah's song (vv. 68–79). And if you're in a closed room that's soundproof, why not sing God a song?...

Confession: A Neglected Art

Confession is probably the most neglected area in personal prayer today. We often hear people pray publicly, "Lord, forgive us for our many sins." A lot of us carry that approach into our private prayer. We throw all our sins onto a pile without so much as looking at them, and we say, "God, please cover the whole dirty heap."

This approach to confession, unfortunately, is a colossal copout. When I lump all my sins together and confess them en-masse, it's not too painful or embarrassing. But if I take those sins out of the pile one by one and call them by name, it's a whole new ball game.

I determined that in my prayers, I would deal with sin specifically. I would say, "I told so-and-so there were nine hundred cars in the parking lot when really there were only six hundred. That was a lie, and therefore I am a liar. I plead for your forgiveness for being a liar."…

I know what will happen to *you* when you have the courage to call your sins by their true names. First, your conscience will be cleansed. "I finally said it," you will think. "I'm finally getting honest with God. I'm not playing games anymore, and it feels good."

Next, you will be flooded with relief that God has a forgiving nature. Knowing that "as far as the east is from the west, so far has he removed our transgressions from us" (Ps 103:12), you will begin to learn the meaning of peace.

Then, you will feel free to pray, "Please give me your strength to forsake that sin from here on out." With the power of the Holy Spirit, you can make a commitment to give up the sin and to live for Christ. And that's when your life begins to show signs of change.

I don't think many of us Christians take confession seriously enough. If we did, our lives would be radically different. When you're totally honest about your sins, something happens. About the fifth day in a row that you have to call yourself a liar, a greedy person, a manipulator or whatever, you say to yourself, "I'm tired of admitting that. With God's power, I've got to root it out of my life."

As God goes to work on your sins, you begin to see Paul's words being fulfilled in your life: "If anyone is in Christ, he is a new creation; the old has gone, the new has come!" (2 Cor 5:17).

Expressing Thanks

The T in ACTS stands for *thanksgiving*. Psalm 103:2 says, "Praise the Lord, O my soul, and forget not all his benefits." Paul writes in 1 Thessalonians 5:18, "Give thanks in all circumstances, for this is God's will for you in Christ Jesus."

Some of us have not made a simple distinction. There is a difference between feeling grateful and expressing thanks. The classic teaching on this is in Luke 17:11–19, the story of the ten men healed of leprosy. How many of those men do you think felt tremendous gratitude as they walked away from Jesus, completely healed of their incurable, disgusting, socially isolating disease? There's no question about it—all ten did. But how many came back, threw themselves at Jesus' feet and thanked him? Just one....

I thank God every day for four kinds of blessings: answered prayers, spiritual blessings, relational blessings and material blessings. Almost everything in my life fits into one of those categories. By the time I've gone through each category, I'm ready to go back to adoration for all God has done for me.

Asking for Help

But then it's time for *supplications*—requests. Philippians 4:6 says, "In everything, by prayer and petition, with thanksgiving, present your requests to God." If you have adored him, confessed your sins and thanked him for all his good gifts, you're ready to tell him what you need.

Nothing is too big for God to handle or too small for him to be interested in. Still, I sometimes wonder if my requests are legitimate. So I'm honest with God. I say, "Lord, I don't know if I have the right to ask for this. I don't know how I should pray about it. But I lift it to you, and if you'll tell me how to pray, I'll pray your way."

God honors that kind of prayer. James says, "If any of you lacks wisdom, he should ask God, who gives generously to all without finding fault, and it will be given to him" (Jas 1:5)....

I break my requests down into categories: ministry, people, family and personal....Break up your requests into whatever categories suit your purposes, and then keep a list of what you've prayed about. After about three weeks, go back and reread your list. Find out what God has already done. In many cases, you will be amazed.

For biographical information on this author, see page 32.

How to Keep a Listening Prayer Journal
LEANNE PAYNE—1994

Although some of the most profound experiences and insights of life come out of keeping track of what we say to God and what we hear Him say, the procedure itself is simple. And it can be an easy "organizational" tool that brings shape and order to everything else we do. The divine order and blueprint lies like a mantle over the lives of those who learn to pray effectively....

To set up your listening prayer journal, start by filling a

loose leaf binder with good-grade paper and five or six dividers....Then order your dividers as follows: Word, Praise and Thanksgiving, Intercession, Petition, Forgiveness.

The bulk of loose-leaf paper is placed after the Word divider, for here we write down those salient points of our daily conversation with God. Prayer starts with and *remains deeply rooted* in the Scriptures; the revealed Word of God quickly discerns our hearts. If our hearts are anxious, fearful, unforgiving, or sinful then they are to be immediately set right in conversation with God. If they are thankful and rejoicing in the work of the day, we will be praising and blessing the Lord, spending more time in intercession for others and personal petition. Whether in joy or in crying out of deep need and utter wretchedness; whether in times of great clarity, the light shining all around; whether in times of confusion, the darkness so oppressive we can barely squeak out our questions before God: all is brought into conversation with Him. The Word section, therefore, is for our daily dialogue with God. This listening to Him "exercises" our spiritual ears to receive the word He sends throughout the day.

The other dividers grant us easy access to prayer lists and the Scriptures and insights that not only pertain to them, but boost our faith and spur us on to prayer. These lists evolve naturally out of our journaling as we receive insight on not only for whom and what to pray but *how* to pray. The Lord yearns to grant us "the Spirit of wisdom and revelation" (Ephesians 1:17) as we continue in prayer. We need only to ask for it. In this way He builds on the previous insights He has given us. These lists often turn into veritable treasure troves. Apart from journaling these insights and listing them for easy access, however, they can become buried treasure—neglected or forgotten altogether.

With dividers and paper in your binder, your pens and pencils at hand, gather up your favorite reference Bible and begin.

I am currently enjoying the New International Version Study Bible with its easy-to-use reference helps, but always have several other translations and commentaries within arm's reach.

In order to neglect no part of the Scriptures, a sound plan for daily Scripture reading is needed....The plan I have used the most is from *The Book of Common Prayer*. It follows the church year: Advent, Christmas, Epiphany, Lent and the Passion of our Lord, the Feasts of the Resurrection, of Ascension, of Pentecost, and then Trinity—the full celebration of God as Father, Son, and Holy Spirit. I prefer the Scripture listings from older versions of this great classic. It is also good to switch plans from time to time. At present, I am enjoying a thematic plan of Scripture reading, *Daily Light from*

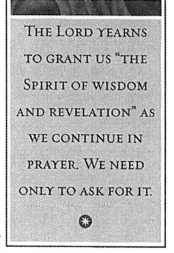

THE LORD YEARNS TO GRANT US "THE SPIRIT OF WISDOM AND REVELATION" AS WE CONTINUE IN PRAYER. WE NEED ONLY TO ASK FOR IT.

the Bible. It employs the King James translation; I read the Scriptures in the NIV as well....

Besides the Scripture readings, I keep several of the great devotional writers' books close at hand. Their meditations on the Scriptures are short and mostly topical, and rarely fail to stimulate. An ancient classic by Thomas á Kempis, *The Imitation of Christ,* and later ones by F. B. Meyer, *Our Daily Walk,* and Oswald Chambers, *My Utmost For His Highest,* are longtime favorites. There are other devotional classics, however, that I simply cannot imagine being without.

As a guide for daily prayer, you may want to type the following out on strong, durable paper and place at the front of your journal:

DAILY PRAYER OUTLINE

I. Meditation on the Scriptures (listening to God through His written word)

II. Praise and Thanksgiving: "Our Father, who art in heaven, hallowed be thy Name."

III. Intercession: "Thy kingdom come, thy will be done, on earth as it is in heaven."

IV. Personal Petitions: "Give us this day our daily bread."

V. Repentance and Forgiveness Prayers: "And forgive us our trespasses, as we forgive those who trespass against us."

VI. A full committal of ourselves and our day to God: "And lead us not into temptation, but deliver us from evil. For thine is the kingdom, and the power, and the glory, forever and ever. Amen."

VII. Listening Prayer

This format for daily prayer can fit into a half-hour prayer time or a full day of prayer. Although we do not need to pray *all* these parts of prayer *every* day, or necessarily in the order given here, they hold within them the principles of a well-rounded prayer-life. This is a way of always praying the prayer Christ taught us.

A prayer journal is not something for anyone else's eyes, and so the matter of guarding the privacy of one's journal must be considered before beginning it. Any "open" prayer journal is unlikely to be a *real* one. Even the fear that someone will invade the privacy of its pages can keep a soul from the searching kind of honesty that should go into it....

The keeping of a prayer journal is so important that I begin it anew each year with a *J.J.* penciled in at the top of the title page and an *S.D.G.* at the bottom. These are Latin initials that stand for the prayer, "Jesus help me," and *"Soli Deo Gloria,"* which means "to the glory of God alone." I learned this from Johann Sebastian Bach, who started and ended his musical compositions in this way. This is how a man of great genius committed his day's work to God.

LEANNE PAYNE is the founder of Pastoral Care Ministries, which conducts seminars and conferences on God's healing grace throughout the United States and

Europe. Among her books are *The Healing Presence, Restoring the Christian Soul,* and *The Broken Image.*

Practicing God's Presence
BROTHER LAWRENCE
OF THE RESURRECTION—*1690*

1. The most holy, common and necessary practice in the spiritual life is the presence of God; that is, habitually to take pleasure in His divine company, speaking humbly and conversing with Him lovingly at all seasons, at every minute, without rule or measure—above all, in the time of temptations, sorrows, dryness, distaste, even of infidelities and sins.

2. One must try continually so that all his actions without distinction may be a sort of little conversation with God; however, not in a studied way, but just as they happen, with purity and simplicity of heart.

3. We must do all our actions with deliberation and care, without impetuosity or precipitation, for these show a disordered spirit. We must work gently, calmly and lovingly with God, and beg Him to accept our work; by this continual attention to God we will break the demon's head and make his weapons fall from his hands.

4. During our work and other actions, even during our reading and writing on spiritual topics, more—during our exterior devotions and vocal prayers—let us stop a few minutes, as often as we can, to adore God in the depths of our hearts, to enjoy

Him, as it were, in passing and in secret. Since you are not unaware that God is present before you during your actions, that He is in the depth and center of your heart, why should you not cease your exterior occupations—at least, from time to time— and even your vocal prayers, to adore Him interiorly, to praise, petition Him, to offer Him your heart, and to thank Him?

What can there be more pleasing to God than thus a thousand times a day to leave all creatures in order to retire and worship Him in one's interior—unless it be to destroy the self-love which can exist only among creatures, of whom we are insensibly freed by these interior returns to God?...

5. All this adoration should be made by faith, believing that God really is in our hearts; that He must be adored, loved and served in spirit and in truth; that He sees all that passes and will pass within us and in all creatures; that He is independent of all, the One upon Whom all creatures depend.

BROTHER LAWRENCE OF THE RESURRECTION (1605–1691) was born Nicholas Herman in Lorraine province, France, and was a soldier and household servant who, after his conversion, entered the religious community of the Carmelites in Paris. There he worked as a helper in the kitchen and became known for his simple, practical faith. He is best known for his book *The Practice of the Presence of God*.

PRAYER

Ask and it will be given to you; seek and you will find; knock and the door will be opened to you. For everyone who asks receives; he who seeks finds; and to him who knocks, the door will be opened.

MATTHEW 7:7–8

During the days of Jesus' life on earth, he offered up prayers and petitions with loud cries and tears to the one who could save him from death, and he was heard because of his reverent submission.

HEBREWS 5:7

✳

CHAPTER 4

A PASSION FOR PRAYER

✵

Vehement Longings after God
JONATHAN EDWARDS—1746

My sense of divine things gradually increased, and became more and more lively, and had more...inward sweetness. The appearance of every thing was altered; there seemed to be, as it were, a calm, sweet cast, or appearance of divine glory, in almost every thing. God's excellency, his wisdom, his purity and love, seemed to appear in every thing; in the sun, moon, and stars; in the clouds, and blue sky; in the grass, flowers, trees; in the water, and all nature; which used greatly to fix my mind. I often used to sit and view the moon for continuance; and in the day, spent much time in viewing the clouds and sky, to behold the sweet glory of God in these things; in the mean time, singing forth, with a low voice my contemplations of the Creator and Redeemer....

I felt then great satisfaction, as to my good state; but that did not content me. I had vehement longings of soul after God and Christ, and after more holiness, wherewith my heart seemed to be full, and ready to break; which often brought to my mind the words of the Psalmist, Psal. cxix. 28. *My soul breaketh for the longing it hath.* I often felt a mourning and lamenting in my heart, that I had not turned to God sooner, that I might have had more time to grow in grace. My mind was greatly fixed on divine things; almost perpetually in the contemplation of them. I spent most of my time in thinking of divine things, year after year; often walking alone in the woods, and solitary places, for meditation, soliloquy, and prayer, and converse with God; and it was always my manner, at such times to sing forth my contemplations. I was almost constantly in ejaculatory prayer, wherever I was. Prayer seemed to be natural to me, as the breath by which the inward burnings of my heart had vent.

JONATHAN EDWARDS (1703–1758) was a pastor and theologian in Northampton, Massachusetts, whose writings on revival established him as the leading spokesman of the revivals that broke out in the 1730s. His many works, including *Some Thoughts Concerning the Revival* and the *Treatise on Religious Affections,* place him in the front ranks of the greatest American theologians. Biography: Ola Winslow, *Jonathan Edwards* (1940).

The Superabundance of the Heart

ANDRÉ LOUF — 1974

Is praying difficult? A fourteenth-century Byzantine monk, who for a short time was Patriarch of Constantinople with the name of Callixtus II, answers this question with the illustration of the lute-player. "The lute-player bends over his instrument and listens attentively to the tune, while his fingers manipulate the plectrum and make the strings vibrate in full-toned harmony. The lute has turned into music; and the man who strums upon it is taken out of himself, for the music is soft and entrancing."

Anyone who prays must set about it in the same way. He has a lute and a plectrum at his disposal. The lute is his heart, the strings of which are the inward senses....To get the strings vibrating and the lute playing he needs a plectrum, in this case: the recollection of God, the Name of Jesus, the Word.

So the lute-player has to listen attentively and vigilantly to his heart and pluck its strings with the Name of Jesus. Until the senses open up and his heart becomes alert. The person who strums incessantly upon his heart with the Name of Jesus sets his heart a' singing, "an ineffable happiness flows into his soul, the recollection of Jesus purifies his spirit and makes it sparkle with divine light."...

We stand now on the threshold of prayer. Our heart has been awakened. It sees Jesus, it hears His voice, it rejoices in

His Word. That Word has been turned over and over in our heart. It has purified us, cleansed us, and we have grown familiar with it. Perhaps we are even beginning to resemble this Word. Now too, it can take root in our heart and bear fruit. Now it may even become the Word of God in our flesh.

So long as we ourselves were still intent on the Word of God in our heart, we had come no further than the prelude. There comes a moment when we yield up God's Word to the Spirit within us. Then it is that our heart gives birth to prayer. And then at last the Word of God has become truly ours. We have then discovered and realized our most profound, our true identity. And then the Name of Jesus has become our name also. And together with Jesus we may with one voice call God: Abba, Father!

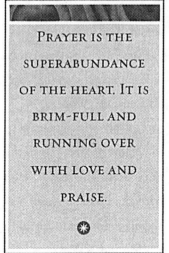

PRAYER IS THE SUPERABUNDANCE OF THE HEART. IT IS BRIM-FULL AND RUNNING OVER WITH LOVE AND PRAISE.

Prayer is the superabundance of the heart. It is brim-full and running over with love and praise, as once it was with Mary, when the Word took root in her body. So too, our heart breaks out into a Magnificat. Now the Word has achieved its "glorious course" (2 Thess. 3:1): it has gone out from God and been sown in the good soil of the heart. Having now been *chewed over* and assimilated, it is regenerated in the heart, to the praise of God. It has taken root in us and is now bearing its fruit: we in our turn utter the Word and send it back to God. We have become Word; we are prayer.

Thus prayer is the precious fruit of the Word—Word of God that has become wholly our own and in that way has been inscribed deep in our body and our psyche, and that now can become our response to the Love of the Father. The Spirit stammers it out in our heart, without our doing anything about it. It bubbles up, it flows, it runs like living water. It is no longer we who pray, but the prayer prays itself in us. The divine life of the risen Christ ripples softly in our heart.

The slow work of transfiguring the cosmos has had a beginning in us. The whole creation has been waiting for this moment: the revelation of the glory of the children of God (Rom. 8:19). It is going on in secret and quite unpretentiously; and yet already in Spirit and truth. We are still in the world, and we dwell already with Jesus near the Father. We still live in the flesh, and the Spirit has already made us wholly captive. For the veil has fallen from our heart, and with unveiled faces we reflect like mirrors the glory and brightness of Jesus, as we ourselves are being recreated in His image, from glory to glory, by His Spirit (2 Cor. 3:18).

So the Word of Christ resides in our heart, in all its richness (Col. 3:16). In it we are rooted, on it we are founded, by it we order our conduct in life, and all the time we overflow with praise and thanksgiving (Col. 2:6–7). This eucharist-thanksgiving has now become our life (Col. 3:15), the superabundance of our heart, the liturgy of the new world that deep within us we already celebrate. We are in fact temples of the Spirit (1 Cor. 6:19).

ANDRÉ LOUF is a member of the Cistercian order and lives in Belgium. He is an experienced teacher of prayer, a sought-after retreat leader, and a specialist in the writings of the Desert Fathers. *Teach Us to Pray* is his best-known work.

Prayer As Wordless Longing
JONI EARECKSON TADA — 1993

Our souls are restless. Raging and thirsting for fulfillment. For pleasure. We find ourselves in a place of wordless longing, always wanting more. And where we place our citizenship, whether in heaven or on earth, is revealed by those things we passionately desire. If we desire dull, sensual things of earth our souls reflect that dullness. But if our desires rise to find fulfillment in the exalted, in the noble, pure, and praiseworthy, then and only then do we find satisfaction, rich and pleasurable.

I'll be the first to admit that such longings heighten my loneliness here on earth. As a citizen of heaven, I know that I am destined for unlimited pleasure at the deepest level. I also know that nothing now quite meets the standards of my longing soul; and that quiet but throbbing ache within me drives me to anticipate heavenly glories above.

Will I miss Bridal Veil falls at Yosemite or the pleasurable taste of a charbroiled chicken Caesar salad? I doubt it. C. S. Lewis says, "Our natural experiences are like penciled lines on flat paper. If our natural experiences vanish in the risen life, they will vanish only as pencil lines vanish from the real landscape; not as a candle flame that is put out, but as a candle flame which becomes invisible because someone has pulled up the blind, thrown open the shutters, and let in the blaze of the risen sun."

Sometimes I get so homesick for heaven that the yearning swells like an ocean wave and I feel as if I'm being swept away, right then and there, to my better heavenly country. I learned long ago that spiritual growth will always include an awakening of these deep longings for heaven, for pleasure at its best. Such an awakening leads to the true contentment of asking less of this life because more is coming in the next.

That's why as a citizen of heaven, if I had a passport, I would copy this poem by William Herbert Carruth on the inside page:

Like tides on a crescent sea-beach,
When the moon is new and thin,
Into our heart's high yearnings
Come welling and surging in—
Come from the mystic ocean,
Whose rim no foot has trod—
Some of us call it Longing,
And others call it God.

Because God has placed powerful longings within you, it stands to reason that He must be the consummation of that need. He directs your longings toward heaven when He commands you to set your heart and mind where Christ is seated above.

At such times—when my prayer has found a place in heavenly glories above—I am at a loss for words. My prayer is more of a silent communion than a long-winded dissertation. Words are unnecessary. Sentences only seem to clutter. My longings are best met when, in prayer, I simply let my heart beat in time with the Lord's.

JONI EARECKSON TADA is the author of many popular books, including *Joni: An Unforgettable Story; Prayers from a Child's Heart; Heaven: Your Real Home;* and *Holiness in Hidden Places.* She is founder and president of Joni and Friends, a Christian outreach to the disability community. She lives in southern California with her husband.

The Syntax of Prayer
RICHARD FOSTER—1992

Loving is the syntax of prayer. To be effective pray-ers, we need to be effective lovers. In "The Rime of the Ancient Mariner," Samuel Coleridge declares, "He prayeth well, who loveth well." Coleridge, of course, got this idea from the Bible, for its pages breathe the language of divine love. Real prayer comes not from gritting our teeth but from falling in love. This is why the great literature on prayer is frankly and wonderfully erotic. "The Trinity," writes Juliana of Norwich, "is our everlasting lover." "O my love!" exclaims Richard Rolle. "O my Honey! O my Harp! O my psalter and canticle all the day!

When will you heal my grief? O root of my heart, when will you come to me?" "Jesus, Lover of my soul," pleads Charles Wesley. "Let me to thy bosom fly."

One day a friend of mine was walking through a shopping mall with his two-year-old son. The child was in a particularly cantankerous mood, fussing and fuming. The frustrated father tried everything to quiet his son, but nothing seemed to help. The child simply would not obey. Then, under some special inspiration, the father scooped up his son and, holding him close to his chest, began singing an impromptu love song. None of the words rhymed. He sang off key. And yet, as best he could, this father began sharing his heart. "I love you," he sang. "I'm so glad you're my boy. You make me happy. I like the way you laugh." On they went from one store to the next. Quietly the father continued to sing off key and making up words that did not rhyme. The child relaxed and became still, listening to this strange and wonderful song. Finally, they finished shopping and went to the car. As the father opened the door and prepared to buckle his son into the carseat, the child lifted his head and said simply, "Sing it to me again, Daddy! Sing it to me again!"

Prayer is a little like that. With simplicity of heart we allow ourselves to be gathered up into the arms of the Father and let him sing his love song over us.

For biographical information on this author, see page 19.

Unceasing Prayer

Thomas R. Kelly—*1941*

There is a way of ordering our mental life on more than one level at once. On one level we may be thinking, discussing, seeing, calculating, meeting all the demands of external affairs. But deep within, behind the scenes, at a profounder level, we may also be in prayer and adoration, song and worship and a gentle receptiveness to divine breathings.

The secular world of today values and cultivates only the first level, assured that *there* is where the real business of mankind is done, and scorns, or smiles in tolerant amusement, at the cultivation of the second level—a luxury enterprise, a vestige of superstition, and occupation for special temperaments. But in a deeply religious culture men know that the deep level of prayer and of divine attendance is the most important thing in the world. It is at this deep level that the real business of life is determined....

Between the two levels is fruitful interplay, but ever the accent must be upon the deeper level, where the soul ever dwells in the presence of the Holy One. For the religious man is forever bringing all affairs of the first level down into the Light, holding them there in the Presence, reseeing them and the whole of the world of men and things in a new and overturning way, and responding to them in spontaneous, incisive and simple ways of love and faith. Facts remain facts, when brought into the Presence in the deeper level, but their value, their significance, is wholly realigned. Much apparent wheat becomes utter chaff, and some chaff becomes wheat. Imposing powers? They are out of the Life, and must crumble. Lost causes? If God be for them, who can be against them? Rationally plausible futures? They are weakened or certified in the dynamic Life and Light. Tragic suffering? Already He is there, and we actively move, in His tenderness, toward the sufferers. Hopeless debauchees? These are children of God, His concern and ours. Inexorable laws of nature? The dependable framework for divine reconstruction. The fall of a sparrow? The Father's love. For faith and hope and love for all things are engendered in the soul, as we practice their submission and our own to the Light Within, as we humbly see all things, even darkly and as through a glass, yet through the eye of God....

How, then, shall we lay hold of that Life and Power, and live the life of prayer without ceasing? By quiet, persistent practice in turning of all our being, day and night, in prayer and inward worship and surrender, toward Him who calls in the deeps of our souls. Mental habits of inward orientation must be established. An inner, secret turning to God can be made fairly steady, after weeks and months and years of practice and lapses and failures and returns. It is as simple an art as Brother Lawrence found it, but it may be long before we achieve any steadiness in the process. Begin now, as you read these words, as you sit in your chair, to offer your whole selves, utterly and in joyful abandon, in quiet, glad surrender to Him who is within. In secret ejaculations of praise, turn in humble wonder to the Light, faint though it may be. Keep contact with the outer world of sense and meanings. Here is no discipline in absent-mindedness. Walk and talk and work and laugh with your friends. But behind the scenes, keep up the life of simple prayer and inward worship. Keep it up throughout the day.

> OUR QUEST IS OF HIS INITIATION, AND IS CARRIED FORWARD IN HIS TENDER POWER AND COMPLETED BY HIS GRACE.

Let inward prayer be your last act before you fall asleep and the first act when you awake. And in time you will find as did Brother Lawrence, that "those who have the gale of the Holy Spirit go forward even in sleep."....

At first the practice of inward prayer is a process of alternation of attention between outer things and Inner Light. Preoccupation with either brings the loss of the other. Yet what is sought is not alternation, but simultaneity, worship undergirding every moment, living prayer, the continuous current and background of all moments of life. Long practice indeed is needed before alternation yields to concurrent immersion in both levels at once. The "plateaus in the learning curve" are so long, and many falter and give up, assenting to alternation as the best that they can do. And no doubt in His graciousness God gives us His gifts, even in intermittent communion, and touches us into flame, far beyond our achievements and deserts. But the hunger of the committed one is for unbroken communion and adoration, and we may be sure He longs for us to find it and supplements our weakness. For our quest is of His initiation, and is carried forward in His tender power and completed by His grace.

THOMAS R. KELLY (1893–1941) was a professor at Haverford College and a Quaker theologian whose work *A Testament of Devotion* has become a spiritual classic. His other works include *The Eternal Promise* and *The Sanctuary of the Soul: Selected Writings by Thomas Kelly*.

Ask, and It Shall Be Given You
ANDREW MURRAY—*1895*

'Ask, and it *shall* be given you; seek, and ye *shall* find; knock, and it *shall* be opened unto you: for every one that asketh *receiveth,* and he that seeketh *findeth;* and to him that knocketh it *shall be opened.*' —Matt. vii. 7, 8

'Ye ask, and *receive not,* because ye ask amiss.' —Jas. iv. 8

Here He wants to teach us what in all Scripture is considered the chief thing in prayer: the assurance that prayer will be heard and answered. Observe how He uses words which mean almost the same thing, and each time repeats the promise so distinctly: 'Ye *shall* receive, ye *shall* find, it *shall* be opened unto you;' and then gives as ground for such assurance the law of the kingdom: 'He that asketh, *receiveth;* he that seeketh, *findeth;* to him that knocketh, *it shall be opened.'* We cannot but feel how in this sixfold repetition He wants to impress deep on our minds this one truth, that we may and must most confidently expect an answer to our prayer. Next to the revelation of the Father's love, there is, in the whole course of the school of prayer, not a more important lesson than this: Every one that asketh, receiveth....

'Ask, and it shall be given you.' Christ has no mightier stimulus to persevering prayer in His school than this. As a child has to prove a sum to be correct, so the proof that we have prayed aright is, *the answer.* If we ask and receive not, it is because we have not learned to pray aright. Let every learner in the school of Christ therefore take the Master's word in all simplicity: Every one that asketh, receiveth. He had good reasons for speaking so unconditionally. Let us beware of weakening the Word with our human wisdom. When he tells us heavenly things, let us believe Him: His Word will explain itself to him who believes it fully. If questions and difficulties arise, let us not seek to have them settled before we accept the Word. No; let us entrust them all to Him: it is His to solve them: our work is first and fully to accept and hold fast His promise. Let in our inner chamber, in the inner chamber of our heart too, the Word be inscribed in letters of light: Every one that asketh, receiveth....

It is one of the terrible marks of the diseased state of Christian life in these days, that there are so many who rest content without the distinct experience of answer to prayer. They pray daily, they ask many things, and trust that some of them will be heard, but know little of direct definite answer to prayer as the rule of daily life. And it is this the Father wills: He seeks daily intercourse with His children in listening to and granting their petitions. He wills that I should come to Him day by day with distinct requests; He wills day by day to do for me what I ask. It was in His answer to prayer that the saints of old learned to know God as the Living One, and were stirred to praise and love (Ps. xxxiv., lxvi. 19, cxvi. 1). Our Teacher waits to imprint this upon our minds: prayer and its answer, the child asking and the father giving, belong to each other.

There may be cases in which the answer is a refusal, because the request is not according to God's Word, as when Moses asked to enter Canaan. But still, there was an answer: God did not leave His servant in uncertainty as to His will. The gods of the heathen are dumb and cannot speak. Our Father lets His child know when He cannot give him what he asks, and he withdraws his petition, even as the Son did in Gethsemane. Both Moses the servant and Christ the Son knew that what they asked was not according to what the Lord had spoken: their prayer was the humble supplication whether it was not possible for the decision to be changed. God will teach those who are teachable and give Him time, by His word and Spirit, whether their request be according to His will or not. Let us withdraw the request, if it be not according to God's mind, or persevere till the answer come. Prayer is appointed to obtain the answer. It is in prayer and its answer that the interchange of love between the Father and His child takes place.

How deep the estrangement of our heart from God must be, that we find it so difficult to grasp such promises. Even

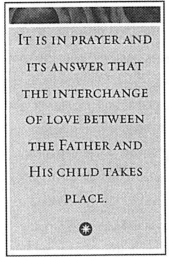

IT IS IN PRAYER AND ITS ANSWER THAT THE INTERCHANGE OF LOVE BETWEEN THE FATHER AND HIS CHILD TAKES PLACE.

while we accept the words and believe their truth, the faith of the heart, that fully has them and rejoices in them, comes so slowly. It is because our spiritual life is still so weak, and the capacity for taking God's thoughts is so feeble. But let us look to Jesus to teach us as none but He can teach. If we take His words in simplicity, and trust Him by His Spirit to make them within us life and power, they will so enter into our inner being, that the spiritual divine reality of the truth they contain will indeed take possession of us, and we shall not rest content until every petition we offer is borne heavenward on Jesus' own words: 'Ask, and it shall be given you.'

For biographical information on this author, see page 14.

Importunity

DAVID HANSEN — 2001

How odd to have to look up a word in a Bible subheading. The subheading names one of Jesus' parables "The Importunate Widow."

I don't use the word *importune*. Yet the words *importune* and *importunity* describe a necessary quality of prayer taught by Jesus himself. Perhaps we dropped the word because it describes extremely unpleasant people. To be importunate is to be burdensome, troublesomely urgent, unreasonably solicitous, overly persistent in request or demand, and rude. In its crudest connotations, to importune can mean to make immoral or lewd advances. We do not like importunate people. They spoil social engagements. They sour work. Importunate parishioners disturb pastors. We do not seek the importunate as friends, we flee them. But God eagerly desires our importunity in prayer....

In Luke's Gospel, Jesus follows the Lord's Prayer with a story about a man whose need requires him to be obnoxious to a friend.

Suppose one of you has a friend, and you go to him at midnight and say to him, "Friend, lend me three loaves of bread; for a friend of mine has arrived, and I have nothing to set before him." And he answers from within, "Do not bother me; the door has already been locked, and my children are with me in bed; I cannot get up and give you anything." I tell you, even though he will not get up and give him anything because he is his friend, at least because of his persistence he will get up and give him whatever he needs. (Lk 11:5–8)

Good prayer is like the relentless knocking and insufferable hollering which can raise a household out of bed and put a man to work in the middle of the night. Even though "he who keeps Israel will neither slumber nor sleep" (Ps 121:4), God asks us to pray as though he must be awakened. As Jesus goes on to say in the same passage: "Ask, and it will be given you; search, and you will find; knock, and the door will be opened for you. For everyone who asks receives, and everyone who searches finds, and for everyone who knocks, the door will be opened" (Lk 11:9–10).

In another place Jesus tells a parable about a widow who will not give up in her demand for her legal rights (Lk 18:1–8)....Obviously, the woman had no money for a bribe and no influential friends or family with which to impress the judge. The only thing the woman could offer the judge was peace and quiet—when he agreed to grant her the justice she deserved.

The woman waited her turn day after day for her opportunity to plead her case. The judge learned to dread her coming. Finally she wore him down. Listen to what the judge says:

"Though I have no fear of God and no respect for anyone, yet because this widow keeps bothering me, I will grant her justice, so that she may not wear me out by continually coming." The phrase "so that she may not wear me out by continually coming" comes from boxing! The verb *hypopiazein* means literally to "hit in the eye."

Jesus is not flattering himself in this parable, nor is he flattering us. He tells us to hit God in the eye with our prayers. He makes God into a stubborn judge and us into pugilistic courtroom lawyers. It may seem unworthy of God. But what seems obnoxious may require supreme faith. Though it may be objectionable to box God in our prayers, the opposite, gracious-delicate prayer is often pathetically self-ingratiating, overcourteous and self-rationalizing before the bar of the god of our personal sensibilities.

A stubborn opponent forces us to think. Required by her circumstances to defend herself with words, the woman in Jesus' parable presented the unjust judge with many arguments. We may surmise that the longer he resisted, the sharper her arguments became. Good prayer forces us to do the same. Thus importunate prayer is theological prayer, not for show or bribe but for the matters of life and death.

DAVID HANSEN is pastor of Kenwood Baptist Church in Cincinnati, Ohio, and the author of *The Art of Pastoring* and *A Little Handbook on Having a Soul*.

Wrestling with God

E. M. BOUNDS — 1895

God conditions the very life and prosperity of His cause on prayer. The condition was put in the very existence of God's cause in this world. *Ask of Me* is the one condition God puts in the very advance and triumph of His cause.

Jesus Christ puts ability to importune as one of the elements of prayer, one of the main conditions of prayer. The prayer of the Syrophenician woman is an exhibition of the matchless power of importunity, of a conflict more real and involving more of vital energy, endurance, and all the higher elements than was ever illustrated in the conflicts of Isthmia of Olympia.

The first lessons of importunity are taught in the Sermon on the Mount: "Ask, and it shall be given; seek, and ye shall find; knock, and it shall be opened." These are steps of advance: "For every one that asketh, receiveth; and he that seeketh, findeth; and to him that knocketh, it shall be opened."

Without continuance the prayer may go unanswered. Importunity is made up of the ability to hold on, to press on, to wait with unrelaxed and unrelaxable grasp, restless desire and restful patience. Importunate prayer is not an incident, but the main thing, not a performance but a passion, not a need but a necessity.

Prayer in its highest form and grandest success assumes the attitude of a wrestler with God. It is the contest, trial and victory of faith; a victory not secured from an enemy, but from Him who tries our faith that He may enlarge it: that tests our strength to make us stronger. Few things give such quickened and permanent vigour to the soul as a long exhaustive season of importunate prayer. It makes an experience, an epoch, a new calendar for the spirit, a new life to religion, a soldierly training. The Bible never wearies in its pressure and illustration of the fact that the highest spiritual good is secure as the return of the outgoing of the highest form of spiritual effort....

Our seasons of importunate prayer cut themselves, like the print of a diamond, into our hardest places, and mark with ineffaceable traces our characters. They are the salient periods of our lives, the memorial stones which endure and to which we turn.

E. M. BOUNDS (1835–1913) was a pastor in Alabama, Tennessee, and Missouri, and served as a chaplain on the front lines with the Confederate Army. He wrote many influential works on prayer, with perhaps the best known being *Power through Prayer*. Biography: Daniel King, *E. M. Bounds* (1998).

Arguing Our Case with God
ISAAC WATTS — 1740

1. We may plead with God from the greatness of our wants, our dangers, or our sorrows; whether they relate to the soul or the body, to this life or the life to come, to ourselves or those for whom we pray. "My sorrows, O Lord, are such as overpress me, and endanger my dishonoring of Thy name and Thy Gospel."

2. The several perfections of the nature of God are another

head of arguments in prayer. "For thy mercies' sake O Lord, save me; thy lovingkindness is infinite, let this infinite loving kindness be displayed in my salvation."

3. Another argument in pleading with God may be drawn from the several relations in which God stands unto men, particularly to his own people. "Lord, Thou art my Creator, wilt thou not have a desire to the work of thine hands?…Thou art my Governor and my King; to whom should I fly for protection but to Thee?"

4. The various and particular promises of the covenant of grace are another rank of arguments to use in prayer. "Enlighten me, O Lord, and pardon me, and sanctify my soul; and bestow grace and glory upon me according to that word of Thy promise on which Thou hast caused me to hope."

5. The name and honor of God in the world is another powerful argument. "What wilt thou do for Thy great name, if Israel be cut off or perish?" (Josh 7:9).

6. Former experiences of ourselves and others are another set of arguments to make use of in prayer. Our Lord Jesus Christ in that prophetical psalm, Psalm 22:5, is represented as using this argument: "Our fathers cried unto Thee, O Lord, and were delivered, they trusted in Thee, and they were not confounded."

7. The most powerful and most prevailing argument is the name and mediation of our Lord Jesus Christ.…"Father we would willingly ask Thee for nothing, but what Thy Son already asks Thee for: we would willingly request nothing at

Thine hands, but what Thine own Son requests before us: Look upon the Lamb, as He had been slain, in the midst of the throne: look upon his pure and perfect righteousness, and that blood with which our High Priest is entered into the highest heavens, and in which for ever He appears before Thee to make intercession; and let every blessing be bestowed upon us, which that blood did purchase, and which that great, that infinite Petitioner pleads for at Thy right hand. What canst Thou deny Thine own Son? For He hath told us, that Thou hearest Him always. For the sake of that Son of Thy love, deny us not."

ISAAC WATTS (1674–1748) was a pastor in London and one of the most popular Christian writers of his time. His books *Improvement of the Mind* (1741) and *The World to Come* (1738) were widely read, but his enduring legacy is as a poet and hymn writer. Beloved hymns include "When I Survey the Wondrous Cross" and "O God, Our Help in Ages Past." See *The Hymns of Isaac Watts*, ed. S. L. Bishop (1962).

Praying for Our Children
STORMIE OMARTIAN — 1995

Praying in the name of Jesus is a major key to God's power. Jesus said, "Most assuredly, I say to you, whatever you ask the Father in My name He will give you" (John 16:23). Praying in the name of Jesus gives us authority over the enemy and proves we have faith in God to do what His Word promises. God knows our thoughts and our needs, but He responds to our prayers. That's because He always gives us a choice about everything, including whether we will trust Him and obey by praying in Jesus' name.

Praying not only affects *us*, it also reaches out and touches those for whom we pray. When we pray for our children, we are asking God to make His presence a part of their lives and work powerfully on their behalf. That doesn't mean there will always be an *immediate* response. Sometimes it can take days, weeks, months, or even years. But our prayers are never lost or meaningless. If we are praying, something is happening, whether we can see it or not. The Bible says, "The effective, fervent prayer of a righteous man avails much" (James 5:16). All that needs to happen in our lives and the lives of our children cannot happen without the presence and power of God. Prayer invites and ignites both.

I actually started praying for each of my children from the time they were conceived because the Bible says, "He has blessed your children within you" (Psalm 147:13). I believed in the power of prayer. What I *didn't* realize at that time was how important each detail of our lives is to Him. It's not enough to pray only for the concerns of the moment; we need to pray for the future, and we need to pray against the effects of past events. When King David was depressed over what had happened in his life and fearful about future consequences (Psalm 143), he didn't just say, "Oh well, whatever will be will be." He cried out to God about the past, present, and future of his life. He prayed about *everything*. And that is exactly what we must do as well.

To do this effectively, I found I had to make an extensive personalized list for each child. This wasn't some legalistic obsession that said, "If I don't pray for each specific detail, God won't cover it." I was simply more at peace when I knew God had heard each of my many concerns. So once a year, when we went to the beach for our family vacation, I used those cherished early morning hours before anyone else was up to spend time with God making a master prayer list. I would sit and gaze out over the ocean, pencil and paper in hand, and ask God to show me how to pray for each child over the next twelve months. After all, He was the only one who truly knew what each child needed and what challenges they would face in the future. The Bible says, "The secret of the Lord is with those who fear Him" (Psalm 25:14). He reveals things to us when we ask. God always met me there with good instructions, and I came home with prayer lists for each of my children. Then, throughout the year, I added to them whenever I needed to do so.

> ALL THAT NEEDS TO HAPPEN IN THE LIVES OF OUR CHILDREN CANNOT HAPPEN WITHOUT THE PRESENCE AND POWER OF GOD. PRAYER INVITES AND IGNITES BOTH.

I kept many of those lists, and as I look back at them now and see all the answers to my prayers, I'm overcome with the faithfulness of God to work in the lives of our children when we pray.

The battle for our children's lives is waged on our knees. When we don't pray, it's like sitting on the sidelines watching our children in a war zone getting shot at from every angle. When we *do* pray, we're in the battle alongside them, appropriating God's power on their behalf. If we also declare the Word of God in our prayers, then we wield a powerful weapon against which no enemy can prevail.

God's Word is "living and powerful, and sharper than any two-edged sword" (Hebrews 4:12) and it pierces everything it touches. God says His Word, "shall not return to Me void, but it shall accomplish what I please, and it shall prosper in the thing for which I sent it" (Isaiah 55:11). In other words, His Word is *never* ineffectual or without fruit....When you are praying for your child, include an appropriate Scripture verse in your prayer. If you can't think of a verse at the moment you're praying, don't let that stop you, but quote a verse or two whenever you can and you'll see mighty things happen.

As you read the Word during your own devotional time and as you pray for your children with the Holy Spirit's leading, you'll find many more Scriptures to include. And you don't have to have a different verse for each prayer. You may have one or two verses that you use repeatedly during a specific season of intercession for your child. For example, when my daughter went through a period of struggle in school, every time we prayed about it together I encouraged her to quote, "I can do all things through Christ who strengthens me" (Philippians 4:13). When I prayed about the matter by myself, I incorporated the verse, "The righteous cry out, and the LORD hears, and delivers them out of all their troubles" (Psalm 34:17).

When we employ God's Word in prayer, we are laying hold of the promises He gives us and appropriating them into the lives of our children. Through His Word, God guides us, speaks to us, and reminds us He is faithful. In that way, He builds faith in *our* hearts and enables us to understand *His* heart. This helps us to pray boldly in faith, knowing exactly what is *His* truth, *His* will, and *our* authority.

STORMIE OMARTIAN is a singer/songwriter and author of *The Power of a Praying Wife, Just Enough Light for the Step I'm On,* and other books. She and her husband, Michael, live in southern California and are the parents of three grown children.

Soldiers of Christ, Arise
CHARLES WESLEY — 1749

Pray, without ceasing pray,
Your Captain gives the word;
His summons cheerfully obey,

And call upon the Lord:

To God your every want

In instant prayer display;

Pray always; pray, and never faint;

Pray, without ceasing pray.

In fellowship alone,

To God with faith draw near;

Approach his courts, besiege his throne

With all the power of prayer:

His mercy now implore,

And now show forth his praise;

In shouts, or silent awe, adore

His miracles of grace.

To God your spirits dart;

Your souls in words declare;

Or groan, to him who reads the heart,

The unutterable prayer:

His mercy now implore,

And now show forth his praise;

In shouts, or silent awe, adore

His miracles of grace.

Pour out your souls to God,

And bow them with your knees;

And spread your heart and hands abroad,

And pray for Zion's peace:

Your guides and brethren bear

Forever on your mind;
Extend the arms of mighty prayer,
In grasping all mankind.

From strength to strength go on;
Wrestle and fight and pray;
Tread all the powers of darkness down,
And win the well-fought day:
Still let the Spirit cry,
In all his soldiers,—Come,
Till Christ the Lord descend from high,
And take the conquerors home.

CHARLES WESLEY (1707–1788), along with his brother John Wesley, was a leader of the Methodist renewal movement in eighteenth-century England. He was a preacher, a great composer of hymns, and a tireless worker among the poor. His classic hymns include "Christ the Lord Is Risen Today," "Soldiers of Christ, Arise," and "Come, Thou Almighty King." Biography: F. L. Wiseman, *Charles Wesley and His Hymns* (1938).

PRAYER

Come, let us bow down in worship,

Let us kneel before the Lord our Maker;

for he is our God

and we are the people of his pasture,

the flock under his care.

Psalm 95:6–7

I want men everywhere to lift up holy hands

in prayer, without anger or disputing.

1 Timothy 2:8

✳

CHAPTER 5

THE
POSTURE
OF
PRAYER

✵

Biblical Prayer Postures
PAUL CEDAR—1998

Scripture refers to a number of other appropriate postures in praying.

Standing. Moses stood on holy ground—without his sandals—as God conversed with him. God said, "Take off your sandals, for the place where you are standing is holy ground" (Exod. 3:5). It is good for us to recognize that whenever we pray, we, like Moses, are standing in the very presence of God.

Abraham stood before the Lord as he pleaded in prayer for God to deliver Sodom. "The men turned away and went toward Sodom, but Abraham remained standing before the Lord" (Gen. 18:22). God heard the prayers of Abraham and made an opportunity for Sodom to be spared.

Lying prostrate. As Ezra praised the Lord, the people bowed down and worshiped the Lord with their faces to the ground.

"Ezra praised the Lord, the great God; and all the people lifted their hands and responded, 'Amen! Amen!' Then they bowed down and worshiped the Lord with their faces to the ground" (Neh. 8:6).

Jesus Himself fell on His face in prayer to His Father in the Garden of Gethsemane. "Going a little farther, he fell to the ground and prayed that if possible the hour might pass from him" (Mark 14:35).

Heads down. From the time of Abraham, servants of the Lord have bowed down in prayer to Him. "When Abraham's servant heard what they said, he bowed down to the ground before the Lord" (Gen. 24:52).

Faces up. Isaiah lifted up his head to see the Lord seated on a throne, high and exalted in the temple. "In the year that King Uzziah died, I saw the Lord seated on a throne, high and exalted, and the train of his robe filled the temple" (Isa. 6:1).

Walking. Before the Fall, Adam walked and talked with God in the Garden of Eden (Gen. 2:8; 3:8–9). Many Christians today are enjoying that same kind of opportunity to commune with God as they walk, often praying for those who live in the houses or apartments they are passing.

Hands folded. Although the Bible does not teach us to fold our hands in prayer, it is a meaningful act for many.

Hands raised. The psalmist wrote about raising his hands to God, both in times of need and in times of praise and worship. "Hear my cry for mercy as I call to you for help, as I lift up my hands toward your Most Holy Place" (Ps. 28:2). "I have seen you in the sanctuary and beheld your power and your glory. Because your love is better than life, my lips will glorify you. I will praise you as long as I live, and in your name I will lift up my hands" (63:2–4). "O Lord, I call to you; come quickly to me. Hear my voice when I call to you. May my prayer be set before you like incense; may the lifting up of my hands be like the evening sacrifice" (141:1–2).

Lying down. The psalmist also wrote about praying when lying in bed. "On my bed I remember you; I think of you through the watches of the night" (63:6). While lying in bed, he communed with God. "I call with all my heart; answer me, O Lord, and I will obey your decrees. I call out to you; save me and I will keep your statutes. I rise before dawn and cry for help; I have put my hope in your word. My eyes stay open through the watches of the night, that I may meditate on your promises" (119:145–148).

Sitting. We can pray when we are sitting, as David did when he prayed for his family and their descendants (2 Sam. 7:18–29).

Our posture helps determine the quality of our prayer times. How we act in the presence of our holy God can enhance or detract from our times of prayer.

The posture of prayer begins with the posture of the heart. Its companions are the posture of humility, the posture of helplessness, and the posture of coming before God with a sense of awe.

PAUL CEDAR for many years pastored churches in Hollywood and Pasadena, California. He is the author of *James, 1–2 Peter, Jude* (Communicator's Commentary) and a widely used course on evangelism, *Sharing the Good Life.*

Postures for Prayer
JEREMY TAYLOR — 1650

Let your posture and gesture of body in prayers be reverent, grave, and humble; according to publike [sic] order, or the best examples, if it be in publick; if it be in private, either stand, or kneel, or lye flat upon the ground on your face, in your ordinary and more solemn prayers; but in extraordinary, casual, and ejaculatory prayers, the reverence and devotion of the soul, and the lifting up of the eyes and hands to God with any other posture not undecent, is usual and commendable; for we may pray in bed, on horseback, *"everywhere, and at all times,"* and in all circumstances: and it is well if we do so; and some servants have not opportunity to pray so often as they would, unless they supply the appetites of Religion by such accidental devotions.

JEREMY TAYLOR (1613–1667) was a prominent Anglican preacher in England during the Puritan revolution. He is most well known for his classic works *The Rule and Exercises of Holy Living* (1650) and *The Rule and Exercises of Holy Dying* (1651).

Present Your Bodies

SIMON TUGWELL — 1974

Very often the body is the most direct way to reach the heart. An embrace speaks more than hundreds of words, a sympathetic look or a gentle touch may do far more to soothe a troubled heart than any amount of more recondite assistance. Similarly our emotions show themselves in our bodies and can to a surprising extent actually be produced or reduced by adopting or changing one's bodily expression. The demarcation between being angry and mimicking anger is not entirely watertight.

So we should not be too coy of just presenting our bodies to God, without undue anxiety about what our hearts and minds are up to. If our minds are too distracted even for vocal prayer, we can still present our bodies in other ways....

[But] we have, by and large, lost our nerve about the intrinsic validity of praying with our bodies. If you go up to someone and shake his hand, you would be very perplexed if he said, "What do you mean?" How on earth would one explain a handshake to someone for whom it was not self-explanatory? We regard the meaning of a handshake as something that looks after itself.

Yet when we read St. Athanasius telling us, in effect, that we are created with hands to pray with, we probably wonder what on earth he means. Yet it was that kind of thing that the early

Christians thought of when they talked about prayer. They did not prescribe mental gymnastics; they just said that we should make the sign of the cross and say the Lord's Prayer; they related how such and such an old monk would spend the whole night standing in prayer with his hands raised and his face towards the place of sunrise. They told how St. James had knees like a camel because he knelt so much.

An Armenian prayer at the beginning of the liturgy contains the petition: "You stretched out your arm in creation even to the stars in the sky: strengthen our arms that our uplifted hands may intercede before you."

We have often been unnecessarily shy about using our bodies to express ourselves. Yet we are told to love God not just with all our heart and mind, but also with all our *soul* (*nephesh* in Hebrew), which means that which makes a body into a living body (Deut 6:4). The vitality of our bodies has its own distinct role in our total relationship with God.

So it need not only be a matter of presenting our bodies before God by just dumping them there like a sack of potatoes, as a last resort when all else fails. Bodily prayer is in itself a valuable part of prayer.

St. Paul tells us to present our bodies as a *living* sacrifice, and surely this indicates that bodily movement and gesture may be involved.... We should notice that kneeling is envisaged as a gesture as well as a posture....

[Among the early Christians], St. Dominic was renowned for his use of the body in prayer. We have an early account called The Nine Ways of Prayer of St. Dominic, which singles out the use of the body as the distinctive Dominican contribution to the doctrine of prayer. It describes the different postures and gestures used by St. Dominic. Sometimes he used to stand on tiptoe, stretching his arms right up towards heaven, like an arrow waiting to be shot up in the air; or he would stand like that with his hands open, as if to catch some blessing from on high; or when he was reading the Bible, he would get tremendously excited and talk and gesticulate as if he were actually with the Lord, face to face.

It is not a matter of borrowing other people's gestures or of making a rubric for our prayer; but of learning to be free to express ourselves in whatever way is most appropriate to ourselves and our circumstances. It is again a matter of learning to use whatever resources we have at the moment.

When you are tired, for instance, it might very well be difficult to become recollected in quiet prayer; but there is nothing to stop you, maybe, going into your room and…kneeling down for a little while, and then, perhaps, prostrating yourself before the Lord. And then perhaps doing it again.

St. Thomas, good Dominican that he was, knew very well that it is often by the use of such bodily gestures of prayer that our hearts come to be drawn to devotion. It is not necessary to do it this way, and it might be impertinent on those occasions when our hearts are already on fire and recollection is easy. But when our hearts are sluggish, it may be best to start with the body. Maybe the heart and mind will come tagging along behind.

And of course it works the other way too. If we are really drawn into prayer with fervour and devotion, then it is likely to seek expression in the body....

God did not make us angels or disembodied spirits, he made us human. And so our prayer should be human. If we confine ourselves always within the limits of strict propriety, we shall be in danger of making prayer unnatural, and then no wonder we shall find it unnaturally difficult. We need not be too shy of expressing ourselves in all the ways that are natural to us. Indeed, as we learn to walk more confidently with the Lord, we may expect to grow in freedom of expression, as part of the glorious liberty of the children of God. This is obviously not a liberty for us to flaunt in self-display or to exercise in disregard of the convenience or even the conventions of others; it must be practiced in simplicity and gentleness.

> IF WE ARE REALLY DRAWN INTO PRAYER WITH FERVOUR AND DEVOTION, THEN IT IS LIKELY TO SEEK EXPRESSION IN THE BODY.

SIMON TUGWELL is Regent of Studies at Blackfriars, Oxford. He teaches theology at Oxford University and also at the Pontifical University of St. Thomas, Rome. His books include *Reflections on the Beatitudes, The Apostolic Fathers,* and *Prayer: Living with God.*

The Body at Prayer
MARTIN L. SMITH — 1989

A starting point is to call into question the minimizing of the role of the body in worship which is so typical of recent western Christianity. In many churches the worshippers' only movements are sitting down, standing up, and bending in an awkward crouching or kneeling position in the narrow confines of a pew. Otherwise all is immobility, except when money is collected. Often worshippers conditioned to these habits carry them over into their private prayer. So the automatic posture of prayer even when they are on their own is to perch against the side of a bed in a hunched-over kneeling position, or to sit in a chair bent forward with elbow on knee and one hand pinching the bridge of the nose. You may not yourself be subject to these automatic attitudes, but you are a fortunate and rare person if you have escaped from the pervasive notion that the role of the body is a minimal one, consisting in "just sitting there."

In order to make the transition into a life of regular meditative prayer most of us need to re-imagine completely what prayer is and can be. And the first principle is that prayer is an activity (and a receptivity!) of the whole person. Or, being more true to our present experience of confusion and divided-ness, prayer is an activity in which all that we are seeks the *gift* of integration and wholeness from God. Prayer is a primal human activity which is falsified when any dimension of our humanness is left behind. If in our communion with God we thwart and exclude part of ourselves, the neglected side of our person will still be present as a saboteur and protester, prevent-ing prayer from really "taking off" or going deep. If we try to leave behind our mind, as some do who launch into prayer seeking to suspend all thinking so as to hear what God will say, we will find that the mind, suddenly starved, will dredge up all manner of inconsequential garbage to work on, so that our silence and stillness is invaded by constant distractions. If we neglect our hearts, the imaginative depths in the self which respond to symbols and images empower our life of feeling, by confining our prayer to thinking religious thoughts and intel-lectualizing about God, prayer remains dry and effortful, an exercise which leaves us unnourished, and unchanged except for the new thoughts we have to add to our collection.

If we do not involve our bodies in prayer, there are several consequences. We may not be able to enter a true, attentive still-ness because our posture frustrates it. Slumped casually on a sofa we become drowsy, kneeling in a tense way we are plagued by pins and needles and restlessness. More than that, we remain inhibited in our self-expression. We use body language and gesture all the time to express ourselves to others. If in prayer we shut down all bodily gesture and movement and confine ourselves to a single position we cut in half our power to feel and own and express our devotion, our love and our needs....

The supreme advantage of praying in true privacy is that we can give free rein to the body to worship. Experiment with simple movements and gestures. Sign yourself with the cross as you stand, very slowly indeed. Repeat the gesture several times with calm dignity. Don't think, don't talk, just feel your body expressing the mystery that you are identified with the crucified Christ, you are one with him, you intend to take up your cross, you live from his self-giving on the cross. As you cross yourself, the body prays all these things. The body knows them. Raise your arms above your head and spread them so that your body takes on the shape of a chalice waiting to be filled. Don't form words, sense your body praying your openness to being filled by God's grace. Feel the dignity and reality of this attitude of receptivity. Let the feeling enacted by your body *be* prayer. Stand, or kneel, and lift your hands out cupped together. Let your body in absolute simplicity pray your needing what God has to give. No need for words! As you pray for others stretch out your hands, palms down in blessing, or make a gesture of offering.

Cross your hands across your heart and bow low. The body is expressing a reverence for the mystery of God that you might not have become aware of through thought alone.

In meditation we can respond to God's touch and word to us through gesture, and by changing our bodily posture to one that expresses the new intention or feeling that we are experiencing. We can also deliberately adopt a posture expressive of a particular attitude or address to God in order to experience it. The importance of this is that our bodies can experience and express faith before, or better than, our thoughts can. A Russian friend of mine tells of an unbeliever in Russia who came to a priest longing to believe in God even though his mind was completely closed to belief as a result of years of indoctrination in atheism. The priest surprised him by making no attempt to argue the case for God. Instead he told his visitor to make a hundred prostrations a day for a month. Prostrations are deep gestures used in the worship of Orthodox Christians. Making the sign of the cross, the worshipper bows deeply touching the floor, or briefly sinks to the ground; this is repeated in a rhythm of reverence. The atheist followed the counsel and found before long that his body was worshipping

> OUR BODIES CAN EXPERIENCE AND EXPRESS FAITH BEFORE, OR BETTER THAN, OUR THOUGHTS CAN.

the God his mind had not yet accepted. Gradually his mind caught up with the truth his body had already grasped and he asked for baptism with immense joy.

For biographical information on this author, see page 85.

Whatever Happened to Kneeling?
DEAN MERRILL—1992

Who can deny that over the past 25 years we have been kneeling less and less? Certain formal occasions still require it, of course: weddings, ordinations, commissioning services for overseas ministry, and the Eucharist in some traditions. Otherwise, we don't kneel before a holy God much anymore. Instead, we face one another and join hands. Kneeling is being replaced by our more interactive, let's share approach to spiritual matters....

Modern sophisms notwithstanding, I still find myself wondering if kneeling doesn't hold some value. When I get down on my knees to pray, the quality of my interaction with God is somehow changed. And I don't think it's just the nostalgic memory of boyhood days when, as a preacher's kid in the Midwest, I knelt on a plank floor with the rest of the congregation at our Wednesday night prayer meetings. I benefit from the practice now.

The biggest benefit is that kneeling reminds us who's who in the dialogue. Prayer is not a couple of fellows chatting about the Dallas Cowboys. It is a human being coming face to face with his or her Supreme Authority, the ineffable God who is approachable but still the One in charge.

Thus, kneeling is a way of saying: "I fully understand who's Boss here. Far be it from me to try to manipulate you or play games with you. I'm well aware of my status in this relationship, and I deeply appreciate your taking time to interact with me."

DEAN MERRILL is publisher of the International Bible Society in Colorado Springs. He is the author or coauthor of many books, including *The God Who Won't Let Go* and *Sinners in the Hands of an Angry Church.*

When the Knee Bends
CALVIN MILLER—2000

When the knee bends, character is born. Not that posture alone is the key to power with God, but it is an indicator of how we see the Almighty. I used to have a prayer partner who began praying on his knees and ended up on his face before God. Why did he do this? His adoration was a malady that only found a cure when he physically humbled himself.

Karl Barth said that prayer is "our longing for Him, our incurable God Sickness." It is a narcosis, an addiction that can never be pleased merely with sipping God when life is born in the swigging.

The knee must bend.

When the knees bend, the King comes! Once when I was in Avila, Spain, I walked into the low stone cell where St. Teresa and St. John of the Cross prayed. The natives of Avila say that they became so engrossed in prayer they levitated. Outlandish? Maybe, though who can know if they did? When we read their work and discover the inherent prostration of their prayers, we can only imagine the glories God bestowed upon their adoration. But I am convinced that the key to God is a bent-knee attitude.

Kneeling should not be seen only as a symbol of devotion. It is far more than that. It is the posture of humility that welcomes the empowering of our lives. When our knees straighten up, we know we must walk again into the fields of service....

KNEELING...IS THE POSTURE OF HUMILITY THAT WELCOMES THE EMPOWERING OF OUR LIVES.

Our whole lives come down in ruin when we live as though we had no knees! I know now the form of a servant is a kneeling form. Consider the things that keep our legs straight. First there is self-sufficiency. We need to learn poverty of spirit. Besides praying, begging is also a kneeling posture. Begging is a pitiful way to make a living—but it is always done with head lower than that of the need supplier. See yourself as poor and you will come to Christ kneeling, and kneeling you will receive....

Narcissism also keeps us from kneeling. Most of our narcissism isn't blatant. In fact, most of us work hard to keep from looking self-centered. We know how to duck our heads and try to look sheepish and yielding if only for the sake of keeping our spiritual reputation. But we are somewhat false. In our public prayer life we cry, "Oh, to be nothing, nothing!" But in our inner lives we cry, "I love meself, I love meself, I pick me up and hug meself."

Remember this: Narcissus was beautiful. The gods all agreed. But...he drowned trying to embrace his own reflection. The metaphor should be a mirror for our pride. Preachers, concert artists, church committee persons, talented church soloists: how many in all these categories live lives serving their own bogus godhood? The apostle's remedy for narcissism was to bend the knee to Christ—a higher God than ego for our needy adoration.

CALVIN MILLER, professor of preaching and pastoral studies at Samford University in Birmingham, Alabama, received his D.M. from Midwestern Baptist Theological Seminary and has served on the editorial boards of such publications as *Leadership* Magazine and *Preaching* Magazine. He is the author of more than forty books, including, the popular *Singer* trilogy, *The Unchained Soul*, and *Once Upon a Tree*.

Recollection

EMILIE GRIFFIN—*2001*

Recollection is a doorway into prayer. It is a kind of focus to arrive at tranquility. This useful practice goes by different names. Sometimes it is called "centering." Richard Foster mentions that the Quakers call it "centering down." Brother Lawrence of the Resurrection speaks of "the practice of the presence." Still another expression is "going within."

An exercise for recollection may go something like this: Right where you are, sit up straight. Put down your notebook, your pencil or anything you have to hold. Make sure your spine is completely straight. Now, relax. Gather yourself in, so to speak. Be completely together in the place where you are. Let any stress or anxiety slide away. Be at peace. Now feel the light of God's presence shining on you, feel God's blessing coming upon you. Accept that blessing. Then breathe in deeply and breathe out deeply. Take one or two breaths, feel the rhythm of it. Next, speak to the Lord, inwardly. You might say to God silently, "Speak, Lord, your servant is listening." Now we have come to the doorway. We are recollected and ready to pray, in fact, we have already begun to pray.

Recollection is a good space to be in at any time. We can move into prayer, or out of prayer, when we are in a recollected state. Recollecting or centering provides an inward attentiveness, or focus, which is essential to all prayer. This practice of gentle concentration moves us into tranquility and peace.

EMILIE GRIFFIN is the author of several books on the spiritual life, including *Clinging: The Experience of Prayer*, *The Reflective Executive*, and *Spiritual Classics*, a collaboration with Richard Foster. She lives with her family in Alexandria, Virginia.

The Place of the Body in Family Worship
MARJORIE J. THOMPSON — 1996

Beyond words, the language of prayer becomes boundless. We have discussed the importance of offering children some symbolic gestures for prayer, such as bowing, kneeling, folding the hands or raising them. While no particular gesture is necessary for God to hear us, many forms of movement might express what is deepest in our hearts. Running, jumping, shouting, or dancing might best convey the exuberance of a child's joy; curling up in a ball or resting one's head in cupped hands might express one child's sadness, while the same gesture might signify peace and contentedness for another child. Children have their own nonverbal language for prayer, which can be encouraged along with verbal prayer forms.

Grown-ups have the same capacity, but it is often more deeply buried and difficult to recover. Most adults have grown extremely self-conscious about movement in worship, being unaccustomed to using the body in prayer and fearful of appearing awkward. Some also fear that particular gestures may identify them with a group whose theology or practice discomforts them. Thus they exclude some of the simplest and most natural movements (such as the raising of hands) and some of the most ancient gestures (such as signing the cross) from the realm of possibility.

One of the beauties of family worship, especially with young children, is the freedom it affords to experiment with bodily participation in prayer. Within the accepting circle of family love, in the relative privacy and informality of family worship, perhaps adults can learn to express their feelings more naturally in prayer, allowing their bodies to help rather than hinder that expression. It might mean something as simple as holding hands, linking arms, or raising one's palms upward in a gesture of receptivity during intercessory prayers. It might mean kneeling together for confession or discovering a unique family gesture for blessing one another. At first, expect that such movement will feel a bit artificial and awkward. But with time and use, the gestures that seem authentic will emerge. No one should be forced in any respect, however. Only as we experience movement's enhancing our worship will we find it freeing.

MARJORIE J. THOMPSON works with the Pathways Center for Spiritual Leadership with Upper Room Ministries in Nashville, Tennessee. She served as a Research Fellow at Yale Divinity School under Henri Nouwen's direction. She is the author of *Soul Feast, Family: The Forming Center*, and many articles in magazines and journals.

Wormwood's Advice

C. S. LEWIS — 1946

My dear Wormwood,

The amateurish suggestions in your last letter warn me that it is high time for me to write to you fully on the painful subject of prayer....

The best thing, where it is possible, is to keep the patient from the serious intention of praying altogether. When the patient is an adult recently converted to the Enemy's party, like your man, this is best done by encouraging him to remember, or to think he remembers, the parrotlike nature of his prayers in childhood. In reaction against that, he may be persuaded to aim at something entirely spontaneous, inward, informal, and unregularised; and what this will actually mean to a beginner will be an effort to produce in himself a vaguely devotional *mood* in which real concentration of will and intelligence have no part. One of their poets, Coleridge, has recorded that he did not pray "with moving lips and bended knees" but merely "composed his spirit to love" and indulged "a sense of supplication." That is exactly the sort of prayer we want; and since it bears a superficial resemblance to the prayer of silence as practised by those who are very far advanced in the Enemy's service, clever and lazy patients can be taken in by it for quite a long time. At the very least, they can be persuaded that the bodily position makes no difference to their prayers; for they constantly forget, what you must always remember, that they are animals and that whatever their bodies do affects their souls. It is funny how mortals always picture us as putting things into their minds: in reality our best work is done by keeping things out....

Your affectionate uncle,

Screwtape

C. S. Lewis (1898–1963) was professor of medieval and renaissance literature at Cambridge University in England. One of the most widely read Christian writers of the twentieth century, he was the author of *Mere Christianity*, *The Chronicles of Narnia*, *The Great Divorce*, *Letter to Malcolm Chiefly on Prayer*, *The Screwtape Letters*, and many other books.

PRAYER

Yet when they were ill, I put on sackcloth
and humbled myself with fasting.
When my prayers returned to me unanswered,
I went about mourning
as though for my friend or brother.
I bowed my head in grief
as though weeping for my mother.

PSALM 35:13–14

When you ask, you do not receive, because you
ask with wrong motives, that you may spend
what you get on your pleasures.

JAMES 4:3

The end of all things is near. Therefore be
clear minded and self-controlled so that you
can pray.

1 PETER 4:7

CHAPTER 6

PROBLEMS
WITH
PRAYER

✵

Resistance to Prayer
HENRI NOUWEN — 1989

Praying is no easy matter. It demands a relationship in which you allow the other to enter into the very center of your person, to speak there, to touch the sensitive core of your being, and allow the other to see so much that you would rather leave in darkness. And when do you really want to do this? Perhaps you would let the other come across the threshold to say something, to touch something, but to allow the other into that place where your life gets its form, that is dangerous and calls for defense.

The resistance to praying is like the resistance of tightly clenched fists. This image shows the tension, the desire to cling tightly to yourself, a greediness which betrays fear.... When you dare to let go and surrender one of those many fears, your hand relaxes and your palms spread out in a gesture of receiving. You must have patience, of course, before your hands are completely open and their muscles relaxed....

Then you feel a bit of new freedom, and praying becomes a joy, a spontaneous reaction to the world and the people around you. Praying becomes effortless, inspired, and lively or peaceful and quiet. Then you recognize the festive and the modest as moments of prayer. You begin to suspect that to pray is to live.

HENRI NOUWEN (1932–1996) taught at Yale Divinity School, Harvard Divinity School, and the University of Notre Dame. From 1986 until his death, he was pastor of the L'Arche Daybreak community in Toronto, Canada. His works include *The Return of the Prodigal Son, The Only Necessary Thing: Living a Prayerful Life,* and *The Wounded Healer.*

Hindrances to Prayer
R. A. TORREY — 1924

There are some things which hinder prayer. These God has made very plain in His Word.

1. The first hindrance to prayer we will find in James 4:3, "Ye ask and receive not *because ye ask amiss, that ye may spend it in your pleasures*" (RV).

A selfish purpose in prayer robs prayer of power. Very many prayers are selfish. These may be prayers for things for which it is perfectly proper to ask, for things which it is the will of God to give, but the motive of the prayer is entirely wrong, and so the prayer falls powerless to the ground. The true purpose in prayer is that God may be glorified in the answer. If we ask any petition merely that we may receive something to use in our pleasures or in our own gratification in one way or another, we "ask amiss" and need not expect to receive what we ask. This explains why many prayers remain unanswered....

2. The second hindrance to prayer we find in Isaiah 59:1–2: "Behold, the Lord's hand is not shortened, that it cannot save; neither his ear heavy, that it cannot hear. But *your iniquities have separated between you and your God, and your sins have hid his face from you, that he will not hear.*"

Sin hinders prayer. Many a man prays and prays and prays and gets absolutely no answer to his prayer. Perhaps he is tempted to think that it is not the will of God to answer, or he may think that the days when God answered prayer, if He ever did, are over....

Many and many a man is crying to God in vain simply because of sin in his life. It may be some sin in the past that has been unconfessed and unjudged, it may be some sin in the present that is cherished, very likely is not even looked upon as sin; but there the sin is, hidden away somewhere in the heart or in the life, and God "will not hear."...

3. The third hindrance to prayer is found in Ezekiel 14:3, "Son of man, these men have taken their idols into their heart, and put the stumbling block of their iniquity before their face: should I be inquired of at all by them?" (RV). *Idols in the heart cause God to refuse to listen to our prayers.*

What is an idol? An idol is anything that takes the place of God, anything that is the supreme object of our affection. God alone has the right to the supreme place in our hearts. Everything and everyone else must be subordinate to Him....

One great question for us to decide, if we would have power in prayer is, Is God absolutely first? Is He before wife, before children, before reputation, before business, before our own lives? If not, prevailing prayer is impossible....

4. The fourth hindrance to prayer is found in Proverbs 21:13, "*Whoso stoppeth his ears at the cry of the poor,* he also shall cry himself, but shall not be heard."

There is perhaps no greater hindrance to prayer than stinginess, the lack of liberality toward the poor and toward God's work. It is the one who gives generously to others who receives generously from God. "Give, and it shall be given unto you; good measure pressed down, shaken together, running over, shall they give into your bosom. For with what measure ye mete it shall be measured to you again" (Luke 6:38, RV). The generous man is the mighty man of prayer. The stingy man is the powerless man of prayer.

One of the most wonderful statements about prevailing prayer...1 John 3:22, "Whatsoever we ask we receive of him, because we keep his commandments, and do those things that are pleasing in his sight," is made in direct connection with generosity toward the needy. In the context we are told that it is when we love, not in word or in tongue, but in deed and in truth, when we open our hearts toward the brother in need, it is then and only then we have confidence toward God in prayer....

5. The fifth hindrance to prayer is found in Mark 11:25, "And when ye stand praying, *forgive*, if ye have ought against any; that your Father also which is in heaven may forgive you your trespasses."

An unforgiving spirit is one of the commonest hindrances to pray. Prayer is answered on the basis that our sins are forgiven; but God cannot deal with us on the basis of forgiveness while we are harboring ill will against those who have wronged us. Anyone who is nursing a grudge against another has fast closed the ear of God against his own petition. How many there are crying to God for the conversion of husband, children, friends, and wondering why it is that their prayer is not answered, when the whole secret is some grudge that they have in their hearts against someone who has injured them....

> GOD CANNOT DEAL WITH US ON THE BASIS OF FORGIVENESS WHILE WE ARE HARBORING ILL WILL AGAINST THOSE WHO HAVE WRONGED US.

6. The sixth hindrance to prayer is found in 1 Peter 3:7, "Ye husbands, in like manner, dwell with your wives according to knowledge, giving honor unto the woman, as unto the weaker vessel as being also joint-heirs of the grace of life; to the end

that your prayers be not hindered" (RV). Here we are plainly told that *a wrong relation between husband and wife is a hindrance to prayer.*

In many and many a case, the prayers of husbands are hindered because of their failures of duty toward their wives. On the other hand, it is also doubtless true that the prayers of wives are hindered because of their failure in duty toward their husband. If husbands and wives should seek diligently to find the cause of their unanswered prayers, they would often find it in their relations to one another....

7. The seventh hindrance to prayer is found in James 1:5–7, "But if any of you lacketh wisdom, let him ask of God, who giveth to all liberally and upbraideth not; and it shall be given him. But let him ask *in faith, nothing doubting*: for he that doubteth is like the surge of the sea driven by the wind and tossed. For let not that man think that he shall receive anything of the Lord" (RV).

Prayers are hindered by unbelief. God demands that we shall believe His Word absolutely. To question it is to make Him a liar. Many of us do that when we plead His promises, and is it any wonder that our prayers are not answered? How many prayers are hindered by our wretched unbelief! We go to God and ask Him for something that is positively promised in His Word, and then we do not more than half expect to get it. "Let not that man think that he shall receive anything of the Lord."

R. A. TORREY (1856–1928) was an evangelist, teacher, and pastor. He served as superintendent of Moody Bible Institute for nineteen years, dean of the Bible Institute of Los Angeles, and pastor of the Church of the Open Door in Los Angeles. He conducted effective evangelistic campaigns around the world, and was the author of many books. Biography: Robert Harkness, *Reuben Archer Torrey: The Man, His Message* (1929).

The Seeming Unreality of the Spiritual Life

DALLAS WILLARD — 1984

[One great barrier to a life in which one hears God's voice is] what Henry Churchill King many years ago called "the seeming unreality of the spiritual life." We could equally well speak of it as "the overwhelming presence of the visible world."

The visible world daily bludgeons us with its things and events. They pinch and pull and hammer away at our bodies. Few people arise in the morning as hungry for God as they are for cornflakes or toast and eggs. But instead of shouting and shoving, the *spiritual* world whispers at us ever so gently. And it appears both at the edges and in the middle of events and things in the so-called real world of the visible....

We are hindered in our progress toward becoming spiritually competent people by how easily we can explain away the movements of God toward us. They go meekly, without much protest. Of course his day will come, but for now he cooperates with the desires and inclinations that make up our character, as we are gradually becoming the kind of people we will forever be. That should send a chill down our spine.

God wants to be wanted, to be wanted enough that we are *ready*, predisposed, to find him present with us. And if, by contrast, we are ready and set to find ways of explaining away his gentle overtures, he will rarely respond with fire from heaven. More likely he will simply leave us alone; and we shall have the satisfaction of thinking ourselves not to be gullible.

The test of character posed by the gentleness of God's approach to us is especially dangerous for those formed by the ideas that dominate our modern world. We live in a culture that has, for centuries now, cultivated the idea that the *skeptical* person is always smarter than one who believes. You can be almost as stupid as a cabbage, as long as you *doubt*. The fashion of the age has identified mental sharpness with a pose, not with genuine intellectual method and character. Only a very hardy individualist or social rebel—or one desperate for another life—therefore stands any chance of discovering the substantiality of the spiritual life today. Today it is the skeptics who are the social conformists, though because of powerful intellectual propaganda they continue to enjoy thinking of themselves as wildly individualistic and unbearably bright.

Partly as a result of this social force toward skepticism, which remains very powerful even when we step into Christian congregations and colleges for ministers, very few people ever develop competence in their prayer life. This is chiefly because they are *prepared* to explain away as coincidences the answers that come to the prayers that they do make. Often they see this as a sign of how intelligent they are. ("Ha! *I* am not so easily fooled as all that!") And in their pride they close off the entrance to life of increasingly confident and powerful prayer. They grow no further, for they have proven to their own satisfaction that prayer is not answered.

Nearly all areas of life in which we could become spiritually competent (hearing God and receiving divine guidance among them) confront us with the same type of challenge. They all require of us *a choice to be a spiritual person, to live a spiritual life.* We are required to "bet our life" that the visible world, while real, is not reality itself.

For biographical information on this author, see pages 35–36.

The Problem of Moods
HARRY EMERSON FOSDICK—*1915*

All of us…have *moods* in which the vision of God grows dim. Our life is not built on a level so that we can maintain a constant elevation of spirit. We have mountains and valleys, emotional ups and downs; and, as with our Lord, the radiant experience of transfiguration is succeeded by an hour of bitterness when the soul cries, "My God, my God, why hast thou forsaken me?" (Matt. 27:46). Cowper tells us that in prayer he had known such exaltation that he thought he would die from excess of joy; but at another time, asked for some hymns for a new hymnal, he wrote in answer, "How can you ask of me such a service? I seem to myself to be banished to a remoteness from God's presence, in comparison with which the distance from the East to the West is vicinity, is cohesion." Of course we cannot always pray with the same intensity and conscious satisfaction. "I pray more heartily at some times than at others," says Tolstoy; and even Bunyan had his familiar difficulties: "O, the starting holes that the heart hath in the time of prayer! None knows how many bye-ways the heart hath and back lanes to slip away from the presence of God."

The first step in dealing with this familiar experience is to recognize its naturalness and therefore to go through it undismayed. When Paul said to Timothy, "Be urgent in season, out of season," he was giving that advice which a wise experience always gives to immaturity: Make up your mind in advance to keep your course steady, *when you feel like it and when you don't.* This difficulty of moods has been met by all God's people. The biography of any spiritual leader contains passages such as this, from one of Hugh Latimer's letters to his fellow-martyr, Ridley: "Pardon me and pray for me; pray for me, I say. For I am sometimes so fearful, that I would creep into a mouse-hole; sometimes God doth visit me again with his comfort. So he cometh and goeth."

A man who surrenders to these variable moods is doomed to inefficiency. He is like a ship that drifts as the tides run and the winds blow, and does not hold its course through them and in spite of them. Matthew Arnold goes to the pith of the problem, so far as duty-doing is concerned:

> tasks in hours of insight willed
> Can be in hours of gloom fulfilled.

And the same attitude is necessary in the life of prayer. Of course we cannot always pray with the same sense of God's nearness, the same warmth of conscious fellowship with him....The heights of fellowship with God are not often reached—even the record of Jesus' life contains only one Transfiguration—but this does not mean that the value of prayer is only thus occasional. As Dean Goulburn put it, *"When you cannot pray as you would, pray as you can."* A man does not deny the existence of the sun because it is a cloudy day, nor cease to count on the sun to serve him and his. Moods are the clouds in our spiritual skies. A man must not overemphasize their importance. Surely he should not on account of them cease to trust the God who is temporarily obscured by them.

Moreover, a man need not passively allow his moods to become chronic. Many a life, like an old-fashioned well, has latent resources of living water underneath, but the pump needs priming. Into a man's prayerless mood let a little living water from some one else's prayer be poured, and water from the nether wells of the man's own soul may flow again. For such a purpose, collections of prayers...are useful; and books of devotion such as St. Augustine's *Confessions*. They often prime the pump. Indeed, prayer itself is a great conqueror of perverse moods. You are not in the spirit of prayer and therefore will refuse to pray until your mood chances to be congenial? But clearly Dr. Forsyth's comparison is apt: "Sometimes when you need rest most you are too restless to lie down and take it. Then compel yourself to lie down and to lie still. Often in ten minutes the compulsion fades into consent and you sleep, and rise a new man...So if you are averse to pray, pray the more."

HARRY EMERSON FOSDICK (1878–1969) was pastor of Riverside Church in New York City, professor of ministry at Union Theological Seminary, and speaker on *National Vespers*, a radio program through which he became known to millions. In addition to *The Meaning of Prayer*, his books include *The Meaning of Faith* and *The Meaning of Service*. Biography: R. M. Miller, *Harry Emerson Fosdick: Preacher, Pastor, Prophet* (1985).

Depend on the Word, Not Feelings
RUTH MYERS—1997

Do you feel at times that your prayers just seem to bounce off the ceiling? Nearly everyone does. Even people who are walking with God with no unconfessed sin in their lives experience this.

Sometimes they feel their prayers are really "getting through"; at other times they feel their words are going nowhere. Are such feelings an indicator of how God views our prayers?

We get in trouble when we depend on our feelings in prayer. We start thinking we have to be in a praying mood to pray, or we call our petitions "good prayers" if they give us a certain feeling. It's much better to just decide to pray as God commands—regardless of how we feel. Charles Spurgeon wrote, "We should pray when we are in a praying mood, for it would be sinful to neglect so fair an opportunity. We should pray when we are not in a praying mood because it would be dangerous to remain in so unhealthy a condition."

It's not that feelings are out of place. Many people, in Bible times and since, have prayed with a deep sense of distress or urgency. The afflicted man in Psalm 102 prayed with loud groaning, "My heart is blighted and withered like grass....I am like a desert owl, like an owl among the ruins." If we have deep troubles, God tells us to pour out our hearts to Him (Psalm 62:8). If He gives us intense concern for others, we're to pray with intense feelings. If He makes us particularly conscious of His presence, let's enjoy it. And if the Spirit carries us along in prayer, let's be grateful. But if not, we can still pray, depending on the Word, like the jet pilot who depends on what the instruments say rather than how he feels. We can't judge the success of our prayers by our emotions. And we're not to let our emotions determine whether or not we pray.

Leaving our feelings in God's hands helps us be more consistent in prayer. If we find ourselves floundering, we can ask the Lord to give us insight as we conduct a "heart checkup":

- Am I yielding to Christ's lordship and abiding in Him?
- Have I confessed every known sin?
- Am I praying in Jesus' name—in His merits and not my own?
- Am I praying in agreement with what I understand to be God's will and purposes?
- Am I praying in faith based on God's Word?

If these checkup questions show that our hearts are right, we can depend on God's promises to hear and answer us. He says in Jeremiah 33:3, "Call to Me, and I will answer you." We can pray "in the Spirit," directed and helped by Him, and depending on the Word He inspired—no matter how we feel....

If you are troubled about an overall lack of positive emotions during prayer, bring your concern to God. Ask Him to overcome any patterns of living or thinking that may be hindering you. But don't get trapped in the error of our feelings-centered age. Feelings are not the only authentic part of our inner person. And being honest in the scriptural sense does not mean expressing all our feelings or responding to all our emotional impulses and preferences. We also have a mind and a will. We can turn our minds to God's commands and with our will choose to obey, even when our feelings don't cooperate.

We please God when we choose to let Him and His Word, rather than feelings, govern us.

Hudson Taylor received amazing answers to prayer. Someone asked him late in life if he always felt joyful when he prayed. He replied that his heart usually felt like wood when he prayed and that most of his major victories came through "emotionless prayer."

Yet our emotions matter greatly to God, and He doesn't ask us to ignore them. When your emotions are unpleasant or absent, don't equate this with sin. Jesus Himself expressed troubled emotions in His prayer life. So tell God how you feel and give your emotions to Him. Then choose to bring Him joy by letting Him, not your feelings, govern your prayer choices.

RUTH MYERS, with her husband, Warren Myers, is the author of *31 Days of Praise* and *31 Days of Prayer*. They have worked with the Navigators in Asia since 1952. They now live in Colorado and travel extensively throughout Asia.

Long Prayer
DAVID HANSEN — 2001

All Christians aspire to long prayer. Some feel it acutely, others barely at all. As sons and daughters of Adam and Eve there is latent in each of us the desire to walk with God in the cool of the evening. As children of Jacob we are required at critical points in our lives to wrestle all night with the angel of the Lord. As those whose spiritual parents trekked with Jesus around Judea, there exists in us the desire to do the same. (I dare say that if the prospect of spending a day wandering the shore of the Sea of Galilee with Jesus of Nazareth is abhorrent to you, you may not be a Christian.) Finally, we need not be children of Enoch to be impressed by the outcome of his life of long prayer: "Enoch walked with God; then he was no more, because God took him" (Gen. 5:24).

Who among us does not long for the personal experience of the apostle Paul's gracious command: "Do not worry about anything, but in everything by prayer and supplication with thanksgiving let your requests be made known to God. And the peace of God, which surpasses all understanding, will guard your hearts and your minds in Christ Jesus" (Phil. 4:6–7). We would gladly unload our anxiety on God and walk away at peace, if we only knew how. It says "pray." Many Christians have tried releasing their worries to God in prayer, but frankly it just hasn't worked. That is, short prayers haven't worked. How can short prayer solve the problem of long worry? It took a long time for anxiety to grip our guts; only long prayer can release that power....

In his Gospel, Mark tells us that "In the morning, while it was still very dark, [Jesus] got up and went out to a deserted place, and there he prayed" (Mk. 1:35). Jesus taught, healed and exorcised demons hour upon hour every day. Whenever he could, he slipped away to a solitary place to pray. He prayed short, and he prayed long. Could he have just prayed short? Would a prayer here and there have kept his compassion furnace stoked for the two-hundredth encounter on a normal day? Could momentary supplications have kept him on the road to the cross? If Jesus needed to leave and pray long to keep his ministry on track, is it possible that we require less? But what does it mean to leave home and go off to a solitary place to pray? He did it. Can we do it?...

Christians who do not pray long because they fail when they try do not know that those who practice long prayer experience the same doomed-attempt feelings. *It must be better for them,* they think. The truth is, it isn't. Most who pray long regularly find their prayers unpretentious and even humiliating. It is embarrassing to spend so much time doing something that feels like nothing. The left hand is hardly tempted to tell the right hand about such paltry offerings. Still, when a fellow believer asks what you did that day, and you tell them simply and honestly that you prayed all day, they imagine that something very different happened to you than happened to them the few times they tried it. They smile approvingly, thinking

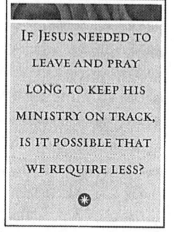

IF JESUS NEEDED TO LEAVE AND PRAY LONG TO KEEP HIS MINISTRY ON TRACK, IS IT POSSIBLE THAT WE REQUIRE LESS?

they can imagine that something great happened, when it really didn't. I don't know how to tell them that I walk around without a destination, talking unconnectedly to an invisible person who answers rarely and then only under the breath....

The familiar rhetoric "What could be more pleasant than spending time with God?" vulgarizes the cross borne in long prayer. Being with God is often unpleasant, not because God is unpleasant. We are insufferable to ourselves. God desires to be with us. But God will not abide with our illusory personas. We can hide no longer. I should think that when a person begins to pray long, he or she might cry a lot. The horribly painful thing about long prayer is being with our self. To pray we must be with our self! Is long prayer anything more than being with our self? It better be. But it cannot be less than that. Long prayer alone can never be less than being with our self. God will settle for nothing less. Maybe that is why God says so little. Maybe Jesus answers infrequently as he waits for us to say an authentic word. Is our unconfessed sin in the way? Yes, to the extent that our unconfessed sin is our unwillingness to know ourselves honestly. Out of love, Jesus will not give us an answer that justifies the specter we see in the mirror. But he will honor us with his presence for hours and years as we search for our true self, so that we can speak an honest sentence—and be healed.

For biographical information on this author, see page 117.

Prayer and Fasting

OLE HALLESBY — 1931

In Mark 9:29 Jesus says, "This kind can come out by nothing, save by prayer and fasting." Here Jesus introduces us to the greatest struggle connected with prayer.

While Jesus and three of the apostles were on the Mount of Transfiguration, a man had brought his son, possessed of a dumb spirit, to the other apostles. The latter had tried to cast out the evil spirit, but they had not succeeded. When Jesus came down, the father brought his son to Him, and Jesus healed the boy. As soon as the apostles had come into the house and were alone with Jesus, they asked Him why they could not cast out the evil spirit. To which Jesus replied, "This kind can come out by nothing, save by prayer and fasting."

Before inquiring into the relationship between prayer and fasting, we must briefly explain what is meant by fasting. To fast is to abstain from eating and drinking for a shorter or longer period of time.

Fasting was enjoined by law in Israel. The whole nation had to fast on a certain day of the year (Lev. 16:29). After the captivity several annual days of fasting were introduced (Zech. 8:19). And the Pharisees went so far that they fasted twice each week (Luke 18:12).

The Hebrew word for fasting signifies the humble submission of the soul to God, the Holy one. For that reason it was observed on the great day of atonement when the people effected their great annual reconciliation with God and otherwise upon occasions of national disaster (Judges 20:26, Joel 2:12, Jonah 3:5) or mourning (1 Sam. 31:13).

Jesus did not abolish fasting; He lifted it from the legalism of the Old Covenant into the freedom of the New. Fasting is an outward act which should be carried out only when there is an inner need of it (Matt. 9:14–15). Furthermore, Jesus warns against fasting as a means of displaying piety, so as to be seen of others (Matt. 6:16–18).

But should *we* fast?

This is no doubt a live question in the minds of many Christians in our day. Many look upon fasting as a part of the outward ceremonialism which belonged only to the Old Covenant. That free, evangelical Christians should fast is entirely strange and foreign to their way of thinking.

So far from the teachings of Jesus and the apostles concerning fasting have we strayed. It is no doubt high time that we feeble, weak-willed and pleasure-loving Christians begin to see what the Scriptures say concerning this element in our sanctification and in our prayer life.

Fasting is not confined to abstinence from eating and drinking. Fasting really means voluntary abstinence for a time from various necessities of life, such as food, drink, sleep, rest, association with people and so forth.

The purpose of such abstinence for a longer of shorter period of time is to loosen to some degree the ties which bind us to the world of material things and our surroundings as a whole, in order that we may concentrate all our spiritual powers upon the unseen and eternal things.

Fasting in the Christian sense does not involve looking upon the necessities of life, which we have mentioned, as unclean or unholy. On the contrary, we have learned from the apostle that nothing is unclean of itself (Rom. 14:14). And that food has been created by God to be received with thanksgiving (1 Tim. 4:3). Fasting implies merely that our souls at certain times need to concentrate more strongly on the one thing needful than at other times, and for that reason we renounce for the time being those things which, in themselves, may be both permissive and profitable.

Fasting is, therefore, entirely in line with...the necessity of having quiet and secluded seasons of prayer, and is in reality only a prolongation of the latter. None of them have been ordained for God's sake, but for our sakes. It is we who need to fast. A great deal could be said about this, but we must limit ourselves to the meaning of fasting in connection with prayer....

The one great secret of prayer is the Spirit of prayer. The most significant thing that we can do in connection with prayer is to establish contact with the Spirit of prayer. To strive in prayer means in the final analysis to take up the battle against all the inner and outward hindrances which would dissociate us from the Spirit of prayer.

It is at this point that God has ordained fasting as a means of carrying on the struggle against the subtle and dangerous hindrances which confront us in prayer.

Fasting must be voluntary, Jesus says.

We Christians resort to fasting when we find that some particular thing is acting as a hindrance to our prayers. This may be some special difficulty of which we are cognizant and which we feel as a hindrance, or it may be something that we do not understand. All we know is that there is something impeding our intercourse with God in prayer.

We resort to fasting in order to set our distracted and worldly-minded souls free for a time from material things and the distraction of our environment, and thus give the Spirit an opportunity to search out our whole inner being and speak with him about the things which are grieving the Spirit of prayer, in order thus to re-establish unhindered communication with the Spirit of prayer and a greater influx of divine power.

For biographical information on this author, see pages 10–11.

When God Is Silent
C. WELTON GADDY — 1995

I used to think that God always answers prayers with either "yes," "no," or "wait a while." (Interestingly, this assumes that all prayers ask something of God.) For a while this simple formula satisfied me. Eventually, though, as I thought about my experiences and listened to stories from other people, I concluded that some prayers receive no specific answer from God. At times, God seems to be deaf to our prayers and silent about answers....

For whatever reasons, most of us experience times when we feel distance and silence between ourselves and God. What should we do when this happens?

Initially, we may find help by carefully examining our personal spiritual situation in light of the possible explanations for God's silence...: Am I failing to hear God because I am not listening, or because God is not speaking? Am I looking for a god which is not God? Do I expect God to conform to my expectations before I accept God's disclosures as revelation?

Honestly, sometimes such introspection yields no beneficial insights. Silence remains.

Carlyle Marney liked to tell people who complained of God's silence to live on the basis of the last clear word from God they heard until they could hear another one. Marney's wise counsel has proven helpful to me. Even during periods of spiritual dryness, God's words from the past remain certain: "I am with you always" (Matt. 28:20); "If we confess our sins, he who is faithful and just will forgive us our sins and cleanse us from all unrighteousness" (1 John 1:9); "Peace I leave with you; my peace I give to you" (John 14:27). I can live for a long time in silence on the basis of those kinds of promises, which I know the silence does not destroy.

When I am not exactly sure what God would have me do in the future, I try to act on what God has instructed me to do in the past: "do justice,…love kindness, and…walk humbly with your God" (Micah 6:8); "be quick to listen, slow to speak, slow to anger" (James 1:19); "love your enemies" (Matt 5:44); "glorify God" (1 Cor. 6:20). Faithful love requires that even when waiting to hear a new word from God, we stay busy trying to carry out the directions God has already given us.

That's the way life goes with lovers. Problems with distance or feelings of distance invade even the most intense love affairs. Sometimes the distance is real, maybe even geographical. In that situation, each lover finds strength and comfort in recalling the words exchanged the last time they were together: "I love you. Being apart cannot destroy my love for you." Memory brings reassurance: "God loves me"; "She loves me."

Emotional distance can be every bit as difficult for lovers to handle as geographical distance. When two people have to negotiate a series of difficult, controversial events, not uncommonly an uneasy feeling of distance develops between them. Faced by this troublesome development, lovers recommit themselves to the kind of communion which contributes to intimacy.

In other situations, one lover feels distance, but the other does not. One asks, "What has happened to us? I don't feel the same closeness between us." The other replies, "I feel as close to you as ever. I don't know why you feel such distance. Maybe you have moved away, but I haven't." At that point, the lovers have to work together to find the source of the sense of separation eating away at one of them.

When distance or silence invades our love affair with God, the need for persistent prayer becomes greater than ever. Honestly negotiating a sense of distance from God (like faithfully proceeding during a period of perceived silence from God) can result in an even more profound love for God.

C. WELTON GADDY is pastor of Northminster Church in Monroe, Louisiana, and the author of numerous books on relationship with God, including *Geography of the Soul, The Gift of Worship,* and *A Love Affair with God.* He has taught at Southern Baptist Theological Seminary, Louisville, Kentucky.

What about Praying to "Daddy"?
BRIAN J. DODD — 1997

Jesus begins the Lord's Prayer with a solemn and respectful approach to God, which is quite different from the extremely popular and widespread misunderstanding that Jesus taught us to pray to God as our "daddy." This mistake is repeated over and over again in books and sermons. It goes like this: "Jesus taught us to pray to *abba,* the Aramaic word for 'daddy.'" This comment is twice wrong, but it is widely believed and is deeply ingrained in popular theology of prayer.

First, the word *abba* is not used in the Lord's Prayer. Matthew uses the Greek for "our Father"...[which] was commonly known in the prayers of Palestinian Judaism of the first century, making it just as likely that Jesus prayed *abhinu* ("our father") as *abba* ("father"). It is misguided to build a case on *abba* when it is not certain that this is the original word Jesus used. There is only one place in the Gospels where it is recorded that Jesus prays to God as *abba*—his prayer in Gethsemane (Mk 14:36, *Abba ho pater;* see Gal 4:6; Rom 8:15). To say that Jesus taught us to pray to our *abba* is not textually grounded.

Second, if *abba* is behind this text (and it may well be), it is most unlikely that it should be translated "daddy." *Abba* is better translated "dear father." "Daddy" was popularized as a translation by Joachim Jeremias in the late 1960s, but his style of argument was flawed, and he later called his own approach "a piece of inadmissible naïveté." Jeremias recanted, and other scholars have refuted his earlier notion. But many preachers and writers have clung to Jeremias's misguided earlier view that *abba* is the chatter of a small child. In a tour de force, Oxford linguist James Barr has shown that Jeremias was mistaken in this now widespread view. *Abba* is best translated with "more a solemn, responsible, adult address to Father." As Barr shows, if "daddy" had been meant, there were Greek words for it. But Matthew, Luke, Mark and Paul did not choose from among those Greek possibilities *(papas, pappas, pappias, pappidion)*. In the three places where *abba* appears in the New Testament, it is immediately translated by a very formal Greek phrase, literally "the Father" *(ho pater;* Mk 14:36; Gal 4:6; Rom 8:15).

Furthermore, the context of the Lord's Prayer supports a more solemn understanding of how Jesus teaches us to address God. The first full sentence of the Lord's Prayer does not take us down the road of childish and individualistic intimacy with God, "my daddy," as we would expect if Jeremias's earlier view were correct. Jesus teaches us to focus on the holiness of God's name and character, and this had to mean for Jesus and his original hearers a focus on the solemn name that God gave to Moses—Yahweh. Jesus teaches us to pray not "my daddy" but "*our* Father, the one in heaven."

We begin prayer with awesome respect for our holy God: "may your holy name be honored." The emphasis is on God's holiness and transcendence, as the second part of the verse clarifies. Prayer, like wisdom, begins with respectful awe for the Lord. Suggesting that we should pray to our "daddy," in addition to being textually unfounded, overlooks the profound emphasis Jesus places on respect for God in the opening of the Lord's Prayer.

Even though *abba* does not mean "daddy," it does remind us that God prizes intimacy with us in prayer. We belong in the throne room of grace, and God is delighted to receive us each time we come. The deep reverence for God with which prayer begins does not minimize the tender relationship God desires with us. We learn from Jesus' teaching and example (not from the word *abba*) that reverence for God is mixed with intimacy; the call to obey God's authority is balanced by the promise of God's mercy and forgiveness. The image of a father in the ancient world usually carried connotations of obedience, provision and mercy. It is no surprise that the Lord's Prayer develops all three: (1) obedience—"your kingdom come, your will be done," (2) provision—"give us this day our daily bread" and (3) mercy—"forgive us our debts, deliver us." Jesus teaches us through the Lord's Prayer and elsewhere that a relationship with God combines respect with intimacy, obedience and forgiveness.

BRIAN J. DODD holds a Ph.D. from the University of Sheffield and serves as pastor of Antioch United Methodist Church in Antioch, California. He is author of *The Problem with Paul* and *Praying Jesus' Way.*

PRAYER

Deep calls to deep
in the roar of your waterfalls;
all your waves and breakers
have swept over me.
By day the Lord directs his love,
at night his song is with me—
a prayer to the God of my life

PSALM 42:7–8

In the same way, the Spirit helps us in our weakness. We do not know what we ought to pray for, but the Spirit himself intercedes for us with groans that words cannot express. And he who searches our hearts knows the mind of the Spirit, because the Spirit intercedes for the saints in accordance with God's will.

ROMANS 8:26–27

✳

CHAPTER 7

POWERLESSNESS

AND

PRAYER

✙

When You Try but Cannot Pray

JOHN BUNYAN—1675

Now some of you may have experienced going in secret and intending to pray and pour out your soul before God, but found that you could scarcely pray anything at all.

Ah! Sweet soul! It is not your words that God so much regards. He will not mind if you cannot come to Him in some eloquent oration. His eye is on the brokenness of your heart; this is what makes the very heart of God to run over. Remember what God promised through David, "The sacrifices of God are a broken spirit; a broken and contrite heart, O God, you will not despise" (Psalm 51:17).

The stopping of your words to God may arise from too much trouble in your heart. David was so troubled sometimes that he could not speak: "I remembered you, O God, and I groaned; I mused, and my spirit grew faint. You kept my eyes from closing; I was too troubled to speak" (Psalm 77:3–4). This might comfort all sorrowful hearts, that though you cannot through the anguish of your spirit speak much, yet the Holy Spirit stirs up in your heart groans and sighs so much more effectively. When your mouth is hindered, with the Holy Spirit your spirit is not hindered. Moses made heaven ring with his prayers, yet not one word came from his mouth in his deepest agony of heart.

> TAKE HEED LEST YOU THINK THAT GOD LOOKS ONLY UPON YOUR WORDS. WHETHER YOUR WORDS BE FEW OR MANY, LET YOUR HEART AND SOUL GO WITH THEM TO GOD.
>
> ✳

If you would more fully express yourself before the Lord, study: first, your filthy estate; second, God's promises; and third, the loving heart of Christ. You may discern the heart of Christ by pondering His condescension and shed blood. You may think of the mercy He has shown to sinners in former times. Then in your prayer plead your own vileness and unworthiness, bemoan your condition before God, plead Christ's shed blood by expostulation, plead for the mercy that He extended to other sinners, plead with His many rich promises of grace, and let these things be upon your heart in your meditations.

Yet, let me still counsel you. Take heed that you do not content yourself with your mere words. Take heed lest you think that God looks only upon your words. Whether your words be few or many, let your heart and soul go with them to God. You shall seek and find Him when you seek Him with your whole heart and being:

> "For I know the plans I have for you," declares the Lord, "plans to prosper you and not to harm you, plans to give you hope and a future. Then you will call upon me and come and pray to me, and I will listen to you. You will seek me and find me when you seek me with all your heart." (Jeremiah 29:11–13)

For biographical information on this author, see page 16.

Rules of Right Praying
JOHN CALVIN — 1536

What then is the first rule of right prayer? Leave behind all thought of our own glory, cast aside all notion of our own worth, put away all self-assurance, humbly giving glory to the Lord. The prophet teaches this: "not on the ground of our own righteousness, but on the ground of Thy great mercy, we pour out our prayers to Thee. Hear us, O Lord, kindly treat us; hear us, do what we ask, for Thine own sake, for over Thy people and Thy holy place is Thy name called upon." Another prophet teaches: "A soul sorrowful, desolate in her great evil, feeble, bowed-down, a soul hungering, her eyes failing, gives glory to Thee, O Lord. Not on the strength of our father's righteousness do we pour out prayers to Thee, beg mercy in

Thy sight, O Lord our God. No—because Thou art merciful, be Thou merciful unto us, for before Thee we have sinned."

Our second rule of prayer is this: Sense our insufficiency we must, earnestly ponder we must how much we need the very things we seek from God; let us then seek them that we may attain them from Him. For with a mind differently intending, feigned and foul our prayer would be. Ask God for forgiveness of sins without knowing yourself the sinner you truly are— what is this but mocking God in your pretending? Ardently, eagerly, ceaselessly seek only what belongs to God's glory. You pray, "Hallowed be Thy name": do this hungering and thirsting after that hallowing of God. Pressed, belabored under the weight of sins, bereft of anything pleasing to God, let us not be terror-struck; rather let us betake ourselves to Him: approach Him we cannot unless we ponder and feel our misery.

God did not set forth prayer haughtily to puff us up before Him or greatly to value our own things. Prayer is for us to confess, weep for our tragic state. As children unburden their troubles to their parents, so it is with us before God. This sense of sin spurs, goads, arouses us to pray.

We know our need to pray, and yet our best of fathers gives us two things to make us seek it more intently: command and promise. Pray, and what you ask you will receive. Seek, come to me, ask me, turn back to me, in the day of need call on me. Take not in vain the name of the Lord. Thus forbidden, we are bidden to hold our God in glory, to lay to His credit all virtue, good, help, protection as we ask of Him these very blessings. Unless when pressed by need we flee to Him, unless we seek Him, beg His help—we draw His anger just as much as those who fashion foreign gods or idols. When we despise all His commands, we are despising His will. But those who call upon Him, seek Him, and give Him praise—theirs is great joy and consolation, for they know thus they render something acceptable to Him and serve His will.

What is His promise? Seek and you will receive, it will be done for you, I'll answer you, rescue you, refresh you, comfort, feed you abundantly; you will not be confounded. Surely all these, promised by God, will be fulfilled if in staunch faith we wait for them. Prayer itself has no worth to merit what it asks: on these promises alone rests, depends the whole hope of prayer. As Peter or Paul or any other saint (though outfitted with greater holiness of life than we) was answered when he prayed, so in our heart of hearts we too must resolve our prayer will be heard—provided in the same staunch faith we call on God. Equipped, armed with the same command to pray, with the same promise our prayer will be answered, we know God weighs our prayer not by our worth but by faith alone. For in faith alone we obey God's commandment and trust His promise.

How goes it with those unsure of God's promise, who call His truth into question, doubt, hesitate over whether an answer will come? Invoking God (as James says), they get nothing. They are waves wind-tossed. Apart from faith nothing can happen to us, for to each according to his faith is given what he asks.

For biographical information on this author, see page 47.

Confessing Helplessness
HENRI NOUWEN — 1972

Often it is said that prayer is simply an expression of help-lessness. It is asking from another what we cannot do ourselves. This is a half truth. The praying person not only says, "I can't do it and I don't understand it," but also, "Of myself, I don't have to be able to do it, and of myself, I don't have to be able to understand it." When you stop at that first phrase, you often pray in confusion and despair, but when you can also add the second, you feel your dependence no longer as helplessness but as joyous openness to others.

If you view your weakness as a disgrace, you will come to rely on prayer only in extreme need and consider prayer as a forced confession of your impotence. But if you see your weakness as that which makes you worth loving, and if you are always pre-pared to be surprised at the power the other gives you, you will discover through praying that living means living together....

To pray is to walk in the full light of God, and to say simply, without holding back, "I am human and you are God." At that moment, conversion occurs, the restoration of the true rela-tionship. A human being is not someone who once in a while makes a mistake, and God is not someone who now and then forgives. No, human beings are sinners and God is love. The conversion experience makes this obvious with stunning simplicity and disarming clarity.

This conversion brings with it the relaxation which lets you breathe again and puts you at rest in the embrace of a forgiving God. The experience results in a calm and simple joy. For then you can say: "I don't know the answer and I can't do this thing, but I don't have to know it, and I don't have to be able to do it." This new knowledge is the liberation which gives you access to everything in creation and leaves you free to play in the garden which lies before you.

For biographical information on this author, see page 152.

The Inadequacy of Our Own Prayers
JAMES HOUSTON — *1996*

[In Psalm 51] David speaks about having a "broken spirit" and a "contrite heart" for the things he has done wrong. We too discover that our own frustrations and sufferings can drive us to rely on God's Spirit rather than on our own resources for strength. Paul writes of this in the New Testament:

The Spirit helps us in our weakness. We do not know what we ought to pray, but the Spirit himself intercedes for us with groans that words cannot express. And he who searches our hearts knows the mind of the Spirit, because the Spirit intercedes for the saints in accordance with God's will.(Romans 8:26–27)

When we are so personally inadequate that we do not know how to express our inner emotions in any rational way, we can only cry out to God, or groan in our frustration....

We groan, as I have known on two important occasions in my own life, when we are wholly frustrated in being able to tell God what our problem or need is. I did not know how I needed help and comfort, or even what to ask from God....

There are other ways in which we can express our inexpressible yearnings to God. We can use the language of the Psalms, allowing them to speak for us when we cannot speak for ourselves:

> As the deer pants for streams of water,
> so my soul pants for you, O God.
> My soul thirsts for God, for the living God.
> When can I go and meet with God?
> My tears have been my food day and night,
> while men say to me all day long,
> "Where is your God?" (42:1–3)

Because prayer is a two-way relationship, we are caught in a deep dilemma. We need to pray to God, but since we are so unlike him, how can we know for certain that he hears us? In fact, the more spiritually aware we become, the deeper this dilemma seems. We start to realize exactly how different our actions and thoughts are from the way God acts and thinks. How can our broken humanity ever express true thoughts and right worship to God? We clearly need the help of the Holy Spirit to grow in true prayer.

Paul can help us here: "He who searches our hearts knows the mind of the Spirit, because the Spirit intercedes for the saints in accordance with God's will." Not only does God's Spirit teach us how to pray, but he prays for us himself....

Another reason why we "groan" in our prayers is that they are so biased toward ourselves and our own view of our needs. This obsession with the self is strong evidence that sin has invaded us as persons.

Self-pity is one of the most subtle ways in which our selfishness expresses itself, for have we not the "right" to be sorry for ourselves when others hurt us? Selfish ambition is another expression of this tendency. Self-display is another, much loved by the Pharisees of Jesus' time. They indulged in attention-seeking even when they thought they were worshiping in the temple. If prayer is "the very soul and essence of religion," as William James put it, then it is only natural that we should groan when our prayers remain so self-preoccupied.

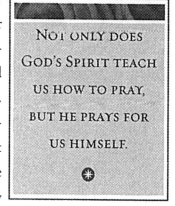

NOT ONLY DOES GOD'S SPIRIT TEACH US HOW TO PRAY, BUT HE PRAYS FOR US HIMSELF.

In the Garden of Gethsemane, hours before his death, Jesus prayed: "Not my will but yours be done." When we can make this prayer our own, then we will have discovered true prayer. This prayer does not mean the destruction of the self, as a Buddhist monk might interpret it, but the true realization of the self as created by God. The self achieves personal communion with God the Father, through the Son, and by the Holy Spirit.

Within the Holy Trinity, each person is for the other. The work and identity of the Holy Spirit is to make the Father and the Son more of a reality in our lives. Because we are made in God's image and likeness, our true identity shines out most strongly when we are relating fully to God and to other people. Selfishness is not just a bit of harmless naughtiness, it is rebellion against the way we were created. It distorts God's intention in creating us as he did, and also his intention of restoring his image in us. The presence of the Holy Spirit in us is therefore vitally important, because he teaches us to pray and relate to God as we were always meant to. As long as we remain in slavery to our self, we will continue to groan in our chains.

For biographical information on this author, see page 62.

The Dark Night of the Soul
SIMON CHAN — 1998

The similarity between growth in prayer and growth in marriage is instructive for anyone seeking a deeper prayer life....Marriage usually starts with a honeymoon period. Many Christians who are converted as adults find that prayer seems to come easily at the beginning of the Christian life. There is little struggle. Temptations are easily overcome. Many obnoxious habits just fall away. Prayer is all enjoyment. Every petition receives an immediate answer. Faith soars. The young lover is experiencing the first flush of romance....

Romance gives way to reality in a period of painful discoveries and adjustments....Praying becomes a constant struggle with distractions. Despite an occasional uplift, one plods through a lifeless devotion. God is silent. It is unfortunate that many modern Christians are never taught such elementary lessons of spiritual progress. They expect their early excitement to continue uninterrupted throughout life. The end of the honeymoon disturbs them, and they seek desperately to rekindle their first flush of feeling. But the great spiritual writers are quite unanimous that this is a basic part of growth. The struggles we have to go through in prayer are part of progress in prayer. There must be purgation, pruning and lancing for certain qualities to develop in preparation for union with God. Masters of the art of prayer try to help us deal with this critical aspect of the prayer life. The most sustained treatment is found in *Ascent of Mount Carmel and The Dark Night of the Soul,* by St. John of the Cross.

The phenomenon of the dark night, so central to the life of

prayer, is little understood nowadays. Some modern Christians see it as a failure instead of a sign of spiritual progress. Their expectations are conditioned by modern sensate culture telling them that whatever is good and true must *feel* good. Christians ought to be joyful and victorious. If they ever feel down, they must be out of God's will....

Against such trivialization of the spiritual life, John's analysis of the dark night takes on special significance. He explains that the dark night begins with the soul who is progressing from the "beginner" to the "proficient" stage. It intensifies with further progress toward union with God. Thus John distinguishes two dark nights—"the night of the sense" and "the night of the spirit." During the first night the soul experiences aridities that tempt it to rely on previous activities that brought joy, namely, meditation and spiritual reflections. But what worked earlier is of no use now. Meditation is done with great dislike and inward unwillingness. The soul must now learn to be quiet and restful, to be patient and to persevere in prayer and not be anxious about meditation, contenting itself with directing its attention lovingly and calmly toward God as it is being led from meditation to contemplation.

The soul that passes through the first night emerges as proficient. It now experiences a new, deeper kind of joy, the joy of infused contemplation, which John describes as "a secret, peaceful and loving infusion of God, which, if admitted, will set the soul on fire with the spirit of love." The proficient experiences "abundant sweetness and interior delight" that come from the sensual part, which is now purified. Still, the purgation of the soul remains incomplete. It must pass through a deeper night, the night of the spirit. Here the soul undergoes further stripping. Sense and spirit are detached from all sweetness and from all imaginations, and the soul travels on the road of faith dark and pure. God denudes the faculties—the affections and feelings, spiritual and sensual, interior and exterior— "leaving the understanding in darkness, the will dry, the memory empty, the affections of the soul in the deepest affliction, bitterness and distress, withholding from it the former sweetness it had in spiritual things."

For John, the dark night is not confined to one phase of the Christian life. It actually intensifies through life as one draws closer to God. But what differentiates a dark night from boredom with life? John makes it clear throughout his work that when one is going through a dark night, however little feeling one has, one continues to persist in prayer, traveling on "the road of faith dark and pure." The less one depends on feelings, the more one is prepared for union with God....

Tragically, unrealistic expectations in regard to the Christian life have kept many modern Christians from accepting the cost of this maturation process. They are like the seeds that fall on stony places. They receive the word with joy—for a time—but when tribulation or persecution comes, they quickly fall away (Mt. 13:20–21). But the soul that perseveres through the dark night comes to the dawn of a new day. A deeper, more mature love emerges. It enjoys a kind of intimacy in prayer that is comparable to the golden years of marriage. Occasional dry spells persist, but they are experienced with aplomb.

SIMON CHAN is a lecturer in systematic theology at Trinity Theological College in Singapore and author of *Spiritual Theology: A Systematic Study of the Christian Life*.

Prayer As Oneness with Christ
MOTHER TERESA — *1991*

In reality, there is only one true prayer, only one substantial prayer: Christ himself. There is only one voice which rises above the face of the earth: the voice of Christ. Prayer is oneness with Christ.

When times come when we can't pray, it is very simple: if Jesus is in my heart, let Him pray, let Him talk to His Father in the silence of my heart. Since I cannot speak, He will speak; since I cannot pray, He will pray.

That's why often we should say, "Jesus in my heart, I believe in your faithful love for me." When we have nothing to give— let us give Him that nothingness. Let us ask Jesus to pray in us, for no one knows the Father better than He. No one can pray better than Jesus, who sends us His Spirit to pray in us, for we do not know how to pray as we ought.

And if my heart is pure, if in my heart Jesus is alive, if my heart is a tabernacle of the living God, Jesus and I are one. As St. Paul has said, "I live—yet no longer I: Christ lives in me."

Christ prays in me, Christ works in me, Christ thinks in me, Christ looks through my eyes, Christ speaks through my words, Christ works with my hands, Christ walks with my feet, Christ loves with my heart....

Prayer is nothing but that complete surrender, complete oneness with Christ. And this is what makes us contemplatives in the heart of the world; for we are twenty-four hours then in His presence: in the hungry, in the naked, in the homeless, in the unwanted, unloved, uncared for.

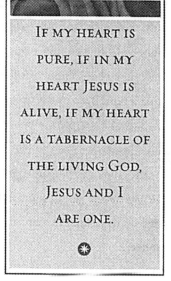

IF MY HEART IS PURE, IF IN MY HEART JESUS IS ALIVE, IF MY HEART IS A TABERNACLE OF THE LIVING GOD, JESUS AND I ARE ONE.

For Jesus said, "Whatever you do to the least of my brethren, you do it to me."

MOTHER TERESA (1910–1997) was born Agnes Gonxha Bojaxhiu to Albanian parents in Skopje, Yugoslavia. She founded the Society of the Missionaries of Charity and spent her life working among the poorest of the poor in

India. She was awarded the Nobel Peace Prize in 1979 and became an honorary citizen of America in 1996. Biography: Malcolm Muggeridge, *Something Beautiful for God* (1986).

Praying in the Spirit

J. OSWALD SANDERS — 1977

There is scriptural warrant for asserting that our chronic disinclination and our reluctance to pray, as well as our ignorance of how to pray aright, find their complete answer in the ministry of the Holy Spirit in our hearts. Hence Paul's injunction, "And pray in the Spirit on all occasions" (Eph. 6:18).

The Holy Spirit is the Source and Sustainer of the spiritual life. "Since we live by the Spirit, let us keep in step with the Spirit" (Gal. 5:25). Since prayer is represented in Scripture as an essential factor in progress in the Christian life, it is not surprising to find that the Spirit of God is deeply involved in this sphere....

In this prayer life, believers have the aid of two Advocates who continually make themselves available and plead our causes. How rich we are through this twofold ministry! The Son of God intercedes for us before the throne of glory, securing for us the benefits of His mediatorial work. "But if anybody does sin, we have one who speaks to the Father in our defense—Jesus Christ, the Righteous One" (1 John 2:1)....

The Spirit of God is Christ's Advocate in our hearts to meet our deepest needs. In announcing the advent of the Holy Spirit, Jesus said, "Unless I go away, the Counselor Helper, Advocate, or Intercessor] will not come to you; but if I go, I will send him to you" (John 16:7). "But you know him, for he lives with you and will be in you" (John 14:17). Paul gives further light on His activity in prayer: "The Spirit himself intercedes for us with groans that words cannot express" (Rom. 8:26)....

Weakness and inadequacy in the art of prayer are not surprising to God. He never intended that prayer should be left to our own unaided faculties. So He gave the Holy Spirit to instruct, inspire, and illumine our hearts and minds. Unaided by Him, we would be likely to pray for things not only contrary to God's will, but injurious to ourselves....

How does the Spirit help us in prayer?

1. It is He who introduces us into the presence of the Father. "For through him we...have access to the Father by one Spirit" (Eph. 2:18). The picture behind *access* is that of a court official introducing people who desire an audience with the king. This is exactly what the Spirit does for us.

2. As the "spirit of grace and supplication" (Zech. 12:10), He overcomes our reluctance, working in us the desire to pray. He graciously, yet faithfully, reveals to us our true heart-needs, and He leads us to seek their fulfillment in prayer.

3. He imparts a sense of sonship and acceptance that creates freedom and confidence in the presence of God. "God sent the Spirit of his Son into our hearts, the Spirit who calls out, '*Abba!* Father!'" (Gal. 4:6). Children are uninhibited in the presence of an understanding and loving father, and so may we be in our prayers.

4. He helps us in the ignorance of our minds and in the infirmities of our bodies, as well as in the maladies of the soul. "In the same way, the Spirit helps us in our weakness. We do not know what we ought to pray for" (Rom. 8:26)....

We can count on the Spirit's aid in guiding us into the will of God by illumining Scripture to us and by stimulating and directing our mental processes. He purifies our desires and redirects them toward the will of God, for He alone knows and can interpret God's will and purpose. "No one knows the thoughts of God except the Spirit of God" (1 Cor. 2:11). He also improves our motivation and inspires confidence and faith in a loving Father.

5. He takes our faltering and imperfect prayers, adds to them the incense of the merits of Christ, and puts them in a form acceptable to our heavenly Father. "Another angel, who had a golden censer, came and stood at the altar. He was given much incense to offer, with the prayers of all the saints, on the golden altar before the throne" (Rev. 8:3). He takes our inarticulate groanings and infuses the right meaning into them.

6. He lays special burdens of prayer on the believer who is

walking sensitively in companionship with Him. Such burdens, intolerable at times, were laid on the prophets; often they could get relief only through prolonged and earnest prayer.

Daniel 10:2–3 refers to one such experience: "At that time I, Daniel, mourned for three weeks. I ate no choice food; no meat or wine touched my lips; and I used no lotions at all until the three weeks were over." But the answer came at the proper time—God's time.

When He lays such prayer burdens on the hearts of His children, He intends to answer the prayer through their intercessions. He will impart the strength to pray through until the answer comes.

J. OSWALD SANDERS, a native of New Zealand, served for many years with the New Zealand Bible Training Institute and the Overseas Missionary Fellowship. His popular writings include *Spiritual Leadership, Effective Prayer,* and *The Incomparable Christ.*

Setting the Will toward God
AMY CARMICHAEL—1945

A few simple *Don'ts* regarding prayer:

Don't be discouraged if at first you seem to get nowhere. I think there is no command in the whole Bible so difficult to obey and so penetrating in power, as the command to be still— "Be still and know that I am God." Many have found this so....

Let the tender understanding of your God enfold you. He

knows the desire of your heart. Sooner or later He will fulfill it. It is written, "He will fulfill the desire of them that fear Him."

Don't feel it necessary to pray all the time; listen. Solomon asked for a hearing heart. It may be that the Lord wants to search the ground of your heart, not the top layer, but the ground. Give Him time to do this. And read the Words of life. Let them enter into you.

Don't forget there is one other person interested in you—extremely interested; he will talk, probably quite vehemently, for there is no truer word then the old couplet,

Satan trembles when he sees

The weakest saint upon his knees.

As far as I know the only way to silence his talk is to read or say aloud (or recall to mind) counter-words, "It is written,…it is written…it is written"; or to sing, for the devil detests song.…

Don't give up in despair if no thoughts and no words come, but only distractions and inward confusions. Often it helps to use the words of others, making them one's own. Psalm, hymn, song—use what helps most.

Don't worry if you fall to sleep. "He giveth unto His beloved in sleep."

And if the day ends in what seems failure, don't fret. Tell Him about it. Tell Him you are sorry. Even so, don't be discouraged. All discouragement is of the devil. It is true as Faber says:

Had I, dear Lord, no pleasure found

But in thought of Thee,

Prayer would have come unsought, and been

A truer liberty.

Yet Thou art most often present, Lord,

In weak distracted prayer;

A sinner out of heart with self

Most often finds Thee there.

For prayer that humbles sets the soul

From all illusions free,

And teaches it how utterly,

Dear Lord, it hangs on Thee.

Then let your soul hang on Him. "My soul hangeth upon Thee"—not upon my happiness in prayer, but just upon Thee. Tell Him you are sorry, and fall back on the old words: "Lord, Thou knowest all things; Thou knowest that I love Thee"—unworthy as I am. Let these words comfort your heart: "The Lord...lifteth up all those that are down."

But maybe it will be quite different. "Sometimes a light surprises the Christian when he sings," or waits with his heart set upon access to his God; and he is bathed in wonder that to such dust of the earth such revelations of love can be given. If so it be, to Him be the praise. It is all of Him.

For biographical information on this author, see page 63.

PRAYER

I urge, then, first of all, that requests, prayers, intercession and thanksgiving be made for everyone—for kings and all those in authority, that we may live peaceful and quiet lives in all godliness and holiness.

1 TIMOTHY 2:1–2

But Jesus often withdrew to lonely places and prayed.

LUKE 5:16

But when you pray, go into your room, close the door and pray to your Father, who is unseen. Then your Father, who sees what is done in secret, will reward you. And when you pray, do not keep on babbling like pagans, for they think they will be heard because of their many words.

MATTHEW 6:6–7

CHAPTER 8

PUBLIC
AND
PRIVATE
PRAYER

❖

Praying in the Five-Fold Form of the Collect

WALTER WANGERIN JR. — 1998

For more than fifteen hundred years a particular kind of prayer has been prayed during worship on the Lord's Day, a prayer that expresses the "collected" thought of an entire congregation with grace and brevity. In fact, it is called the Collect. We have and we continue to use hundreds of collects, ancient and modern. Their humility of spirit is balanced by certainty of faith. They span the full breadth of human need. They are filled with the goodness of the Gospel and with a constant sense of the support and the presence of the whole community of Christians.

The perfect collect is both strong and beautiful. It comes in the easy language of common people, but it is shaped by a wise and teaching *form*. It is this form which can guide us also into a wisdom of faithful praying.

Many of us have learned to pray spontaneous prayers of supplication and thanksgiving. We pray the words that spring immediately to our lips: need shapes them, or the mood of the moment, or overwhelming feeling. Surely, this is our speaking unto God. It is righteous prayer.

But over time we may discover that our personal praying has fallen into a narrow rut of repetition, that our prayer-thought and our words are in fact more limited than our faith and our love, that we have so much more to *say* to God than our prayers are capable of containing.

Christian, have you paid attention lately to the focus of your prayers? Do you center mostly upon yourself?—what you need?—what you hope for?—what you desire (even lovingly) for those around you? Well, but there are *two* engaged in this communication. God is the other. Does God *as God* receive as much attention and detail as you grant yourself in your prayer? Do your topics of conversation relate mostly to the little you, neglecting the endlessly various Lord, about whom so much can be said?

Then learn the form which our wise forbears in the faith developed.

Use your own words! It shall in every respect be your speech unto the dear Lord God. But as you honor and obey the five separate parts of the Collect, you will (1) turn spontaneous cries into serious and thoughtful conversation with God, (2) find your attention drawn more and more to the very source and life of your faith and praying and (3) discover such a richness of petition that it *will* be capable of expressing the true complexity of your heart and mind.

Here is an example of a very old collect, this one praying for our purity before the Lord. I will divide it according to its five parts so that you might see how seamlessly one leads into the next:

Invocation Almighty God,

Basis for petition unto whom all hearts are open, all desires known, and from whom no secrets are hid:

Petition Cleanse the thoughts of our hearts by the inspiration of your Holy Spirit,

Purpose that we may perfectly love you and worthily magnify your holy name;

Ending through Jesus Christ, your Son, our Lord. Amen.

Any prayer on any occasion—whether private or familial or public—can be prayed according to these parts, and the one praying shall be moved farther and farther from self, closer and closer to God.... The very form of this prayer has led us in utter sentiments higher than we might have been capable of on our own. This is what it means to pray with the whole Christian Church on earth, even if not another human soul is near to hear what we are saying.

For biographical information on this author, see page 44.

The Purpose of Public Prayer
CHARLES G. FINNEY — 1835

One of the purposes of assembling several persons together for united prayer is to promote union among Christians. Nothing tends more to cement the hearts of Christians than praying together. Never do they love one another so well as when they witness the outpouring of each other's hearts in prayer.

Public prayer enables believers to extend the spirit of prayer. God has so constituted us, and such is the economy of His grace, that we are sympathetic beings and communicate our feelings to one another. Nothing is more calculated to promote a spirit of prayer than to unite with someone who has the spirit of prayer, unless this one should be so far ahead of others that his prayer repels the rest. His prayer should awaken others and encourage them to join in the spirit of intercession.

Another grand design of social prayer is to move God. Not that prayer necessarily changes the mind and feelings of God, but when the prayer of faith is offered by Christians, it behooves God to bestow the answer.

A united prayer meeting also serves to convict and convert sinners. Sinners are apt to be solemn when they hear Christians pray. Where there is a spirit of prayer, they feel there is something more. As soon as Christians begin to pray as they ought, sinners will sense the weight of their sins. They do not understand what spirituality is because they have no experience of it, but when Christians pray in faith, the Spirit of God is poured out and sinners are broken down and often converted on the spot....

The prayer meeting is an index to the state of spirituality in a church. If the prayer meeting is neglected or the spirit of prayer is not manifested, you know, of course, that spirituality is at low ebb. I can enter a prayer meeting and know the spiritual state of a church.

Every minister should know that if the prayer meetings are neglected, all his labors are in vain. Unless he can get Christians to attend the prayer meetings, all else that he can do will not improve their state of spirituality.

A great responsibility rests on the one who leads a prayer meeting. If the meeting is not what it ought to be, if it does not elevate the spirituality of the participants, he should seriously search out to see what the problem is and get the spirit of prayer back. He should also prepare himself to make appropriate remarks calculated to motivate and set things right. A leader who is not prepared both in head and heart has no business leading a prayer meeting.

Prayer meetings are the most important meetings in the church. It is highly important for Christians to sustain prayer meetings in order to (a) promote union, (b) increase brotherly love, (c) cultivate Christian confidence, (d) promote their own growth in grace, and (e) cherish and advance spirituality.

Prayer meetings should be so numerous in the church, and

be so arranged, as to exercise the gifts of every member—man or woman. Everyone should have the opportunity to pray and to express the feelings of his heart. Sectional prayer meetings are designed to do this. And if they are too large to allow it, let them be divided so as to bring the entire group into the work, to exercise all gifts, and diffuse union, confidence, and brotherly love, through the whole.

CHARLES G. FINNEY (1792–1875) was the leading revivalist in nineteenth-century America and became known as the "Father of Modern Revivalism." He served as a pastor in New York and Ohio, as professor of theology, and as president of Oberlin College. His writings include "Lectures on Revivals of Religion" and "Lectures on Systematic Theology." Biography: Keith Hardman, *Charles Grandison Finney: Revivalist and Reformer* (1987).

Public and Private Prayer
JOHN CALVIN—1536

Such constancy in prayer applies to private devotion, but not to the public prayers we offer in the church. Such are not constant and are to be given only by the common consent of all. Paul's words "decently and in order" mean that certain convenient hours are humanly agreed upon, appointed, accommodated to the need of all—but not divinely set. "Temples" we call the public places appointed for such rites. No secret temple-sanctity makes prayers more holy or causes them to be heard by God. A temple is but to accommodate the believing congregation as it gathers to pray, to hear the Word preached, to take the sacraments. "True temples of God," says Paul, "are we." Do you wish to pray in God's temple? Pray in yourself. Like Jews and pagans are those who think God's ear comes closer in a temple, or fancy their prayer more holy by the holiness of the place. Such physical worship goes against the words of John: "Worship God in spirit and in truth"—think not of place. And so, because the goal of prayer is to arouse and bear our hearts to God (praising or beseeching), the essence of prayer is set in mind and heart; or better said: prayer is an emotion of the heart within, poured out, laid bare before God, searcher of hearts.

Christ told us the best way to pray: "In your bedroom, with door closed, pray in secret to your Father, that He who is in secret may hear you." No prayer of hypocrites, vainly, showily grasping after men's favor, is this call to secret prayer. And so Christ bids us descend into our hearts with our whole thought, promises us God will be near us in the affection of our hearts, entempled in our bodies. Pray you may in other places too, but prayer is something secret, lodged chiefly in the heart, requiring tranquility far from all teeming cares.

Voice and song interposed in prayer must spring from one's deepest heart. To pray with the lips alone or from the throat is to abuse God's holy name, deride His majesty, and bring down His wrath. In the prophet's words He speaks: "With their mouth the people draw near to Me, with their lips honor Me, but far from Me are their hearts; and it is by the command and teaching of men that they have feared Me. A marvelous miracle will I do among this people: the wisdom of their wise shall perish; the prudence of their elders shall vanish."

And so speaking and singing must be tied to the heart's affection, must serve it. Shifty, slippery, inattentive is the mind toward thinking of God unless exercised by prayerful speech and song. The glory of God ought to shine in the various parts of our bodies, and especially in the tongue, created to sing, speak forth, tell, proclaim the praise of God. And the tongue's chief task is, in the public prayers offered in the assembly of believers, with one common voice, with a single mouth, to glorify God together, to worship Him together in one spirit, one faith. Openly, mutually we receive our brother's confession and are in turn by his example to give our own.

Not in Greek among Latins, not in Latin among French or English, but in the daily language, understood by the whole assembly, are public prayers to be voiced. Edify thus the whole church: a sound not understood cannot benefit. Not moved to this by love? Let Paul then tell you clearly: "How can the unlearned say amen to your blessing by the spirit if he is ignorant of what you are saying? Unedified is he by your giving thanks."

Private or public—tongue-prayers without the mind are not heard by God. In fact the force and ardor of the mind must outstrip whatever the tongue in speaking can express. One final word: in private prayer no tongue is needed, for inner feeling will suffice to rouse us to the best, the silent prayer, as Moses and Hannah knew.

For biographical information on this author, see page 47.

Catching Fire
JIM CYMBALA — 1997

"Welcome back, Pastor Cymbala," people said when they saw me that morning. "Did you have a good rest in Florida? How's your cough?"

I told them my cough was much better, but inside, I couldn't wait to tell them something far more important. Early in the service I said, "Brothers and sisters, I really feel that I've heard from God about the future of our church. While I was away, I was calling out to God to help us—to help *me*— understand what he wants most from us. And I believe I've heard an answer.

"It's not fancy or profound or spectacular. But I want to say to you today with all the seriousness I can muster: *From this day on, the prayer meeting will be the barometer of our church. What happens on Tuesday night will be the gauge by which we will judge success or failure because that will be the measure by which God blesses us.*

"If we call upon the Lord, he has promised in his Word to answer, to bring the unsaved to himself, to pour out his Spirit among us. If we don't call upon the Lord, he has promised nothing—nothing at all. It's as simple as that. No matter what I preach or what we claim to believe in our heads, the future will depend upon our times of prayer.

"This is the engine that will drive the church. Yes, I want you to keep coming on Sundays—but Tuesday night is what it's really all about. Carol and I have set our course, and we hope you'll come along with us."…

If my announcement to that congregation sounds strange and overbearing, consider that it was not a whole lot different from what Charles Haddon Spurgeon, the great British pulpiteer, had said in a sermon almost exactly a hundred years before:

> The condition of the church may be very accurately gauged by its prayer meetings. So is the prayer meeting a grace-ometer, and from it we may judge of the amount of divine working among a people. If God be near a church, it must pray. And if he be not there, one of the first tokens of his absence will be a slothfulness in prayer.

That first Tuesday night, fifteen to eighteen people showed up. I had no agenda or program laid out; I just stood up and led the people in singing and praising God. Out of that came extended prayer. I felt a new sense of unity and love among us. God seemed to be knitting us together. I didn't preach a typical sermon; there was new liberty to wait on God's presence.

In the weeks that followed, answers to prayer became noticeable. New people gradually joined, with talents and skills that could help us. Unsaved relatives and total strangers began to show up. We started to think of ourselves as a "Holy Ghost emergency room" where people in spiritual trauma could be rescued....

So week after week, I kept encouraging the people to pray....

We were not there to hear one another give voice to eloquent prayers; we were too desperate for that. We focused vertically, on God, rather than horizontally on one another. Much of the time we called out to the Lord as a group, all praying aloud in concert, a practice that continues to this day. At other times we would join hands in circles of prayer, or various people would speak up with a special burden to express.

> IF WE CALL UPON THE LORD, HE HAS PROMISED IN HIS WORD TO ANSWER....IF WE DON'T CALL UPON THE LORD, HE HAS PROMISED NOTHING....IT'S AS SIMPLE AS THAT.
>
> ✳

The format of a prayer meeting is not nearly as important as its essence—touching the Almighty, crying out with one's whole being. I have been in noisy prayer meetings that were mainly a show. I have been with groups in times of silent prayer that were deeply spiritual. The atmosphere of the meeting may vary; what matters most is that we encounter the God of the universe, not just each other.

I also began to ease up in the Sunday meetings and not control them so tightly with a microphone. The usual format—two songs, then announcements, special music by the choir, the offering, then the sermon, finally a benediction—was gradually laid aside as God began to loosen me up. I didn't have to be so nervous or uptight—or phony. I had only been protecting myself out of fear.

After all, people weren't hungry for fancy sermons or organizational polish. They just wanted love. They wanted to know that God could pick them up and give them a second chance.

In those early days on Atlantic Avenue, as people drew near to the Lord, received the Spirit's fullness, and rekindled their first love for God, they naturally began to talk about it on their jobs, in their apartment buildings, at family gatherings. Soon they were bringing new people.

From that day to the present, more than two decades later, there has never been a season of decline in the church, thank God. By his grace we have never had a faction rise up and decide to split away. God has continued to send people who need help; often I can't even find out how they learned of us.

JIM CYMBALA has been pastor of the Brooklyn Tabernacle, Brooklyn, New York, for thirty years. During that time the congregation has grown from twenty members to more than six thousand; the Tuesday night prayer meeting continues to serve as the focus and hub of congregational life. Jim's books include *Fresh Wind, Fresh Fire, Fresh Faith,* and *Fresh Power.*

The Symphony of Prayer
GEORGE A. BUTTRICK — 1942

"Can't a man pray without belonging to a church?" He cannot pray well or fully until he is a member of some fellowship of prayer. "But isn't prayer in its nature private?" No, nothing is in its nature wholly private: it is both private and corporate. Jesus advised us to pray in secret in an inner chamber with the door shut. That counsel remains, for every man's heart is still a moated castle. But Jesus taught also a group worship: "Where two or three are gathered together in my name"—or two or three hundred—"there am I in the midst of them" [Matt. 18:20]. He said the Temple should be "called of all nations the house of prayer" [Mark. 11:17]. That counsel also remains, for the moated castle of man's heart draws its stones from common ground, and its moat-water comes from a common river of life. Corporate prayer is not a process of addition—one added to one added to one until every worshiper is counted. It is a process of multiplication: a divine electricity flashes from every life: there are endless "commutations" of the Spirit. Corporate prayer is not an aggregate: it is a symphony. "Where nine or ten are gathered in holiness," said an old Jewish proverb, "there is the majesty of God." So Jesus prayed on the mountainside all night alone. But he prayed also in the synagogue and Temple, and in the little group of his disciples. We need community. When an earthly group betrays us, we must build new communities of home, toil, art, nationhood, and the world....In these new commonwealths we must live and love, lest the paralysis of egocentricity should slay us. But, because every community is "devoured by Time's devouring hand," we must be joined to a Higher Community, "where neither moth nor rust doth corrupt, and where thieves do not break through nor steal" [Matt. 6:20]. The fulfillment of our nature is in corporate prayer.

GEORGE A. BUTTRICK (1892–1980) was an English-born Congregational preacher who served nearly thirty years as pastor of New York's Madison Avenue Presbyterian Church. He served as Preacher to the University at Harvard and was named as one of the top ten preachers of the twentieth century by *Preacher* magazine.

The Trinity and Public Prayer
THOMAS C. ODEN — 1983

The liturgist needs a firm grasp of the ways in which the acts of prayer correlate with the heart of Christian doctrine, namely, the Christian teaching about the triune God. Nothing is more uniquely a mark of the Christian understanding of God than the notion that the one God is Creator, the Father whose son Jesus came to us with redemption and forgiveness as incarnate Lord, crucified and risen, and out of the Father and the Son proceeds the Holy Spirit who evokes, guides, comforts, challenges, and empowers the community of celebration. The triune God, who is incomparably One in these three persons, is similarly present in unifying diverse acts of prayer.

The public worship...must itself be clearly understood by the pastor. There are three phrases or clusters of motifs that recur—usually in sequence—that need to be clearly grasped by the liturgical leader.

- awe/invocation/adoration/thanksgiving—the opening sequence of acts
- confession/repentance/supplication/affirmation of faith/witness—the central sequence of acts of worship
- grateful responsiveness/dedication/oblation/commitment to the Christian life—the concluding sequence of acts of common prayer

These three liturgical acts...constitute a meaningful order that makes up a wholesome and well-ordered act of worship. The service proceeds from a sense of awe fitting to God's holiness and mystery, toward thanksgiving and praise, which itself tends toward radical self-examination in which we become aware of our sin and guilt and in repentance bring ourselves before the divine mercy. Then true repentance becomes the proper basis upon which the contrite person can hear the good news of God's forgiveness, so as to be able conscientiously to utter the affirmation of faith that rehearses the story of God's self-giving in Jesus Christ. Our response in offertory and bene-diction is to offer ourselves as God has offered himself to us.

This, in summary form, is what happens in Christian worship. This threefold sequence of worship is implicitly triune. The oft-discussed distinction between "types of prayer" correlates with the triune doctrine of God....Our thesis: prayer is an oft-enacted sequence of approaches and responses to God that correspond to the reality of God as Father, Son, and Spirit....

Prayer to God the Father

In prayer we meet God first in the consciousness of awe, a due sense of reverence for God as unsearchable mystery, incomparable goodness, and insurmountable power. The holy God evokes in us a sense of reverence that remains "the beginning of wisdom" (Ps. 111:10). We know ourselves to be radically dependent upon this mysterious and transcendent reality. That is the opening mood of prayer in the Jewish and the Christian traditions. Adoration only ascribes to God the glory that is God's due. It says to God, "You are so different from all else in our experience that we can only sit in amazement. We ask for nothing but simply to worship You."

It is this adored reality that we call upon and beseech to be present with us in our worship. We collect together and present ourselves before God. We invoke God's name, inviting God to make his living presence known and felt among us. The moving language of the Anglican collect for Holy Communion concisely grasps this approach: "Almighty God, unto whom all hearts be open, all desires known, and from whom no secrets are hid; cleanse the thoughts of our hearts by the inspiration of thy Holy Spirit, that we may perfectly love thee, and worthily magnify thy holy Name; through Christ our Lord. Amen."

We offer our praise and thanksgiving to the Creator God not only for the goods of creation but also for their source in the insurmountable divine goodness. Thanksgiving in due course is addressed to God the creator, God the redeemer, and God the sanctifier (Father, Son, Spirit; beginner, mediator, fulfiller). We begin by thanking the creator for our lives, continue by thanking the redeemer for our salvation, and conclude by thanking God the Spirit for the ongoing work of sanctification, even until the end of time.

Prayer to God the Son

We have taken the good creation and with our free will abused it, seeking lesser goods, exalting limited values as if they were absolutes, falling away from the greatest good so as to find ourselves ever more deeply enmeshed in adoring limited goods. The result is social, historical, political, and personal sin that is primordially engendered, intergenerationally mediated, and unawarely received. In confession, we hold up before God precisely this alienated human condition. We know that we have strayed like lost sheep, followed too much the devices and desires of our own hearts, and left undone those things that we ought to have done, and that there is no health in us. We petition earnestly for God's mercy and forgiveness.

The Christian service of worship remembers the good news of Jesus Christ, and in its light, we pray for the pardon made known through the Son. The Affirmation of Faith, that God the Father has met us through his Son Jesus Christ, includes Scripture reading, creed and sermon, and the hearing the word read, confessed, and exposited. The written word is spoken aloud from the law, prophets, psalms, and apostles. The creed is a condensed statement of the rule of faith in the triune God implicit in the baptismal formula. The homily then seeks to make clear to the contemporary believer that God the Father has come to us in his Son Jesus Christ to offer us newness of life, forgiveness, freedom, and love.

Prayer to God the Spirit

This then calls for another turn in the sequence of prayer. Having received the gospel, the prayers of the faithful are addressed to God the Spirit, who wills to complete the work begun in the Father and dramatically revealed in the Son, so as to finish the work of redemption that was needed because of the fallenness of creation. The prayer for sanctification essentially exists as a response to the gospel, asking for guidance of the Spirit to enable us to respond fittingly.

Here we pray in the mode of petition. We ask God to purify our hearts and to bless our human efforts. Petition may take the form of asking for illumination, for God's presence to be with us as we listen to Scripture so that we may discern its meaning clearly. We pray that God the Spirit may work effectually in our hearts. Petition may come not only in the form of supplication (petition for oneself) but also of intercession (petition for others). We intercede on behalf of those imprisoned, sick, lonely, alienated, and not for individuals only but for collective distortions in both the church and society. We especially intercede for those who are radically vulnerable: the poor, those in dire need, the dying, the bereaved. Their suffering is viewed and beheld in direct relation to God's own suffering for us. Bidding prayers may intercede for someone or something in particular: for God's grace to be poured upon a marriage or on a new life coming into being or for comfort amid loss.

All of this leads to the prayer of oblation or dedication, when we offer ourselves to God in response to God's offering of himself to us. The benediction symbolizes the return into the world with God's strength and blessing to embody his love to the world as it has been embodied to us in Christ.

This then reveals an implicit trinitarian design embedded in common prayer. It is called common because, as distinguished from private prayer, it occurs in community, in common with other believers. The minister who does not understand this order may be confusing the congregation. Its inner structure is best grasped in relation to the center of ancient ecumenical orthodoxy: God is one, Father, Son, and Holy Spirit. If the service jumps awkwardly backward from pardon to the concern for penitence, or from oblation to awe, the triune sequence has lost its unity and become confused, and the faithful believer senses something amiss. If the liturgist fixates on one part of that sequence to the neglect of the other aspects, the inner logic of the service becomes distorted. Christian worship proceeds from awe through pardon to dedication, and from God the Father through the Son to the inspiration of the Spirit. This pattern of prayer correlates with the creator who gives us life, the redeemer who brings us back to the original purpose of life when fallen, and the Spirit who sanctifies and completes what is offered and given in Christ.

THOMAS C. ODEN is a Methodist minister and professor of theology at Drew University in New Jersey. He is the author of a major systematic theology in three volumes: *The Living God, The Word of Life,* and *Life in the Spirit.* Other writings include *Doctrinal Standards in the Wesleyan Tradition* and *The Care of Souls in the Classic Tradition.*

Solitude, Not Privacy

EUGENE H. PETERSON — *1985*

Solitude in prayer is not privacy. The differences between privacy and solitude are profound. Privacy is our attempt to insulate the self from interference; solitude leaves the company of others for a time in order to listen to them more deeply, be aware of them, serve them. Privacy is getting away from others so that I don't have to be bothered with them; solitude is getting away from the crowd so that I can be instructed by the still, small voice of God, who is enthroned on the praises of the multitudes. Private prayers are selfish and thin; prayer in solitude enrolls in a multi-voiced, century-layered community: with angels and archangels in all the company of heaven we sing, "Holy, Holy, Holy, Lord God Almighty."

We can no more have a private prayer than we can have a private language. A private language is impossible. Every word spoken carries with it a long history of development in complex communities of experience. All speech is relational, making a community of speakers and listeners. So too is prayer. Prayer is language used in a community of the Word—spoken or read, understood and obeyed (or misunderstood and disobeyed). We can do this in solitude, but we cannot do it in private. It involves an Other and others.

The self is only *itself*, healthy and whole, when it is in relationship, and that relationship is always dual, with God and with other human beings. Relationship implies mutuality, give and take, listening and responding.

For biographical information on this author, see page 56.

Learn to Be Alone
Thomas Merton — 1961

Physical solitude, exterior silence and real recollection are all morally necessary for anyone who wants to lead a contemplative life, but like everything else in creation they are nothing more than means to an end, and if we do not understand the end we will make a wrong use of the means.

We do not go into the desert to escape people but to learn how to find them; we do not leave them in order to have nothing more to do with them, but to find out the way to do them the most good. But this is only a secondary end.

The one end that includes all others is the love of God.

How can people act and speak as if solitude were a matter of no importance in the interior life? Only those who have never experienced real solitude can glibly declare that it "makes no difference" and that only solitude of the heart really matters! One solitude must lead to the other!

However, the truest solitude is not something outside you, not an absence of men or of sound around you; it is an abyss opening up in the center of your own soul. And this abyss of interior solitude is a hunger that will never be satisfied with any created thing.

The only way to find solitude is by hunger and thirst and sorrow and poverty and desire, and the man who has found solitude is empty, as if he had been emptied by death.

He has advanced beyond all horizons. There are no directions left in which he can travel. This is a country whose center is everywhere and whose circumference is nowhere. You do not find it by traveling but by standing still.

Yet it is in this loneliness that the deepest activities begin. It is here that you discover act without motion, labor that is profound repose, vision in obscurity, and, beyond all desire, a fulfillment whose limits extend to infinity.

Although it is true that this solitude is everywhere, there is a mechanism for finding it that has some reference to actual space, to geography, to physical isolation from the towns and the cities of men.

There should be at least a room, or some corner where no one will find you and disturb you

> THE TRUEST SOLITUDE IS NOT... AN ABSENCE OF MEN OR OF SOUND AROUND YOU; IT IS AN ABYSS OPENING UP IN THE CENTER OF YOUR OWN SOUL.
>
> ✳

or notice you. You should be able to untether yourself from the world and set yourself free, loosing all the fine strings and strands of tension that bind you, by sight, by sound, by thought, to the presence of other men.

"But thou, when thou shalt pray, enter into thy chamber, and having shut the door, pray to thy Father in secret...."

Once you have found such a place, be content with it, and do not be disturbed if a good reason takes you out of it. Love it, and return to it as soon as you can, and do not be too quick to change it for another.

City churches are sometimes quiet and peaceful solitudes, caves of silence where a man can seek refuge from the intolerable arrogance of the business world. One can be more alone, sometimes, in church than in a room in one's own house. At home, one can always be routed out and disturbed (and one should not resent this, for love sometimes demands it). But in these quiet churches one remains nameless, undisturbed in the shadows, where there are only a few chance, anonymous strangers among the vigil lights, and the curious impersonal postures of the bad statues. The very tastelessness and shabbiness of some churches makes them greater solitudes, though churches should not be vulgar. Even if they are, as long as they are dark it makes little difference.

Let there always be quiet, dark churches in which men can take refuge. Places where they can kneel in silence. Houses of God, filled with His silent presence. There, even when they do not know how to pray, at least they can be still and breathe easily. Let there be a place somewhere in which you can breathe naturally, quietly, and not have to take your breath in continuous short gasps. A place where your mind can be idle, and forget its concerns, descend into silence, and worship the Father in secret.

There can be no contemplation where there is no secret.

THOMAS MERTON (1915–1968), one of the most influential spiritual writers of the twentieth century, spent twenty-seven years at a Trappist monastery in Kentucky, during which time he wrote nearly fifty books, including his widely read autobiography, *The Seven Storey Mountain.* Other influential works include *Contemplation in a World of Action, The Wisdom of the Desert,* and *Thoughts in Solitude.*

PRAYER

Pray also for me, that whenever I open my mouth, words will be given me so that I will fearlessly make known the mystery of the gospel, for which I am an ambassador in chains. Pray that I may declare it fearlessly, as I should.

EPHESIANS 6:19–20

Is any one of you sick? He should call the elders of the church to pray over him and anoint him with oil in the name of the Lord. And the prayer offered in faith will make the sick person well; the Lord will raise him up. If he has sinned he will be forgiven. Therefore confess your sins to each other and pray for each other so that you may be healed. The prayer of righteous man is powerful and effective.

JAMES 5:14–16

CHAPTER 9

PASTORAL
PRAYER

✷

Prayer and Preaching
E. M. BOUNDS — *1890*

Almost the last words uttered by our Lord before His ascension to heaven, were those addressed to the eleven disciples, words which, really, were spoken to, and having directly to do with, preachers, words which indicate very clearly the needed fitness which these men must have to preach the Gospel: "But tarry ye in the city of Jerusalem," says Jesus, "til ye be endued with power from on high."

Two things are very clearly set forth in these urgent directions. First, the power of the Holy Ghost for which they must tarry. This was to be received after their conversion, an indispensable requisite, equipping them for the great task set before them. Secondly, the "promise of the Father," this "power from on high," would come to them after they had waited in earnest, continuous prayer. A reference to Acts 1:14 will reveal that these same men, with the women, "continued with one accord in prayer and supplication," and so continued until the Day of Pentecost, when the power from on high descended upon them.

This "power from on high," as important to those early preachers as it is to present-day preachers, was not the force of a mighty intellect, holding in its grasp great truths, flooding them with light, and forming them into verbal shapeliness and beauty. Nor was it the acquisition of great learning, or the result of an address, faultless and complete by rule of rhetoric. None of these things. Nor was this spiritual power held then, nor is it held now, in the keeping of any earthly sources of power....The transmission of such power is directly from God, a bestowal, in rich measure, of the force and energy which pertains only to God, and which is transmitted to His messengers only in answer to a longing, wrestling attitude of his soul before his Master, conscious of his own impotency and seeking the omnipotency of the Lord he serves....

> THE TRANSMISSION OF POWER IS DIRECTLY FROM GOD, A BESTOWAL, IN RICH MEASURE, OF THE FORCE AND ENERGY WHICH PERTAINS ONLY TO GOD.

The "power from on high" may be found in combination with all sources of human power, but is not to be confounded with them, is not dependent upon them, and must never be superseded by them. Whatever of human gift, talent or force a preacher may possess it is not to be made paramount, or even conspicuous. It must be hidden, lost, overshadowed by this "power from on high." The forces of intellect and culture may all be present, but without this inward, heaven-given power, all spiritual effort if is vain and unsuccessful....

Preachers of the present age excel those of the past in many, possibly in all, human elements of success. They are well abreast of the age in learning, research, and intellectual vigour. But these things neither insure "power from on high" nor guarantee a live, thriving religious experience, or righteous life. These purely human gifts do not bring with them an insight into the deep things of God, or strong faith in the Scriptures, or an intense loyalty to God's divine revelation.

The presence of these earthly talents even in the most commanding and impressive form, and richest measure do not in the least abate the necessity for the added endowment of the Holy Spirit. Herein lies the great danger menacing the pulpit of to-day. All around us we see a tendency to substitute human gifts and worldly attainments for that supernatural, inward power which comes from on high in answer to earnest prayer....Oh, that the present-day ministry may come to see that its one great need is an enduement of "power from on high," and that this one need can be secured only by the use of God's appointed means of grace—the ministry of prayer.

For biographical information on this author, see page 119.

The Minister's Role in Prayer
THOMAS C. ODEN — 1890

According to most Protestant interpretations of priesthood, the minister is no longer an offerer of sacrifice to God according to the Levitical pattern, because that has already adequately occurred in Jesus Christ. So what remains for the Christian minister to do in the priestly office? The Christian minister representatively intercedes on behalf of the faithful community before God in prayer as a timely, public, verbal, hearable act. To illustrate:

In the pew sits an elderly woman who has lost her son, yet who does not fully understand that loss and cannot articulate its depth. It is not that God needs her prayer in order to hear her, but rather that she needs to hear better articulated what she already feels in her heart. But if she, more than God, needs the ministry of prayer, it is also clear that God invites it and responds to it. Ministry seeks to offer language for the prayer in her heart.

Next to her sits a young man with gutter-low self-esteem, who has felt dozens of opportunities slip by, who now feels an unspecific anxiety about his ability to cope with any daily task. He comes to the service of Christian worship unconsciously needing to interpret himself before God but hardly knowing how to take the first step. He needs someone to help him enter into the presence of God. The pastor as representative liturgist leads the community in prayer, and in doing so enables and facilitates their own praying. Pastoral prayer does not eclipse or diminish the prayers of the laity, but rather, hopes to engender them and breathe into them new life.

Behind him is a young woman who is struggling with real guilt tinged with elements of hidden neurotic guilt. She knows that she has been cold and cruel to one about whom she deeply cares. She is aware of her inadequacy, but needs someone to interpret it in the presence of God, to offer prayer for forgiveness in a personally significant way so as to relieve and transform the real guilt, and help her understand the neurotic guilt. She comes to the gathered church to hear that prayer spoken, even though she could not have told you that in advance.

In the back row is a person who has slipped in late, feeling a bit awkward, who did not even know until the service began that he needed someone to interpret for him, as if standing before God, a recent moment of intense joy and aesthetic fulfillment. He discovers to his amazement that he needed a worshiping community with a representative ministry to place his deep joy in the context of a larger sense of the joy of God over creation.

This is what ministry does: says these things openly, offers these prayers fittingly, gives praise for the community heartily, offers God's forgiveness to the contrite—calling all to lively response to the power of grace. To receive this priestly service is in large part why people come to church.

Priestly ministry seeks to give language, form, symbol, and expression to these otherwise unspoken human experiences, by offering them symbolic interpretation in a community of prayer. By analogy, only because Christ knew what was in human hearts was he prepared to be priest to humanity. By empathetically sharing in our human condition, entering our fleshly sphere of suffering, even unto death, Christ came to know who we are, so as to interpret us before God. Pastorally this suggests a deep analogy between God's incarnate love and the care of souls.

The Christian ministry follows this incarnational pattern of Christ in entering into the depths of human experience, seeking to understand it, not be self-deceptive about it—to penetrate its masks, not ignoring its limits or evil dimensions. In the service of worship we hold all this human amalgam up before the Lord. This beholding-interceding activity occurs not just on Sunday, but throughout the hourly encounters of each week. Only the minister who has visited, who knows the people, who is in touch with their hurts, hopes, and possibilities, can on Sunday morning pray believably for the whole people. The pastor who has been immersed in the lives of the people daily is then ready to carry these needs, aspirations, and longings before God in prayer and before the gathered community by means of homily.

For biographical information on this author, see page 222.

Prayer As Pastoral Care
JOHN W. FRYE — 2000

We all require a setting in which we can express our needs, be transparent, and receive the love and pastoring of Jesus through *"his body"*—other brothers and sisters in Christ. My wife and I are very thankful to be part of a loving small group in which we exuberantly worship, pray for and receive prayer from others, practice the gifts of the Spirit, and, frankly, can just "be." This kind of "house church" experience is vital for pastoral survival.

Our house church meeting usually includes singing some praise and worship songs accompanied by CD. We can sing as loud and as long as we want. We can bow down, kneel, clap, and dance. We can shout, cry, and be silent....Then we may spend time in prayer, adoring God, blessing his name, and recounting his great qualities and deeds. We may move into a time of listening prayer in which someone receives a "word," sees a "picture," or senses an impression from God. In the security and trust of the house church, we are free to explore what it means for Jesus to literally be among us and communicate his heart to us.

One evening a "picture" came to one of the older and wiser members of our group. He said, "Does anyone see the key, like the key to a member's windup toy on Mike's back? I believe God is telling Mike (not his real name) that he has all kinds of stress in his life. He's feeling like a machine just going through the motions. God wants to bring to Mike supernatural peace."

Mike was floored. This was his first time to meet this older Christian. Mike operates a heart-lung machine while surgeons do open-heart surgery (an occupation permeated with stress). Mike was also tangled in a messy process of trying to sell his home and simplify his family's life (even more stress). He felt exactly like a toy wound tight, moving mechanically through life. The picture couldn't have been more accurate.

We put Mike on the "prayer bench," gathered around him, and began intercessory prayer. That night Mike knew that God loved him with a special, specific love, and Mike knew that God was on his side, for him, not against him.

You can't help but be renewed, refreshed, "pastored" in settings like that....

The pastoral adventure is learning to perceive and report the Lord Jesus' walking-in-our-midst presence. It may be quiet and ordinary, or it may be unusual and full of tears or laughter. Through the faithful practice of the disciplines, through the obedient use of spiritual gifts, through faith that activates all our capacity to perceive him, pastoring is bringing God to people. Our Chief Shepherd did just that. God visited us as the Word incarnate. As undershepherds our calling is the same.

JOHN W. FRYE has served as teaching pastor at Bella Vista Church in Rockford, Michigan, for the past eighteen years. He holds a D.Min. from Fuller Theological Seminary and is the author of *Jesus the Pastor: Leading Others in the Character and Power of Christ.*

Leading Public Prayer
GEORGE A. BUTTRICK—1942

Corporate prayer is the heart of corporate worship. Ritual is not central; for, however necessary and vital, it is still ritual. Scripture is not central; for, however indispensable and radiant, it is still scripture—that which is written, the record not the experience, the very word but not the Presence. Preaching is not central; for preaching, however inevitable and kindling, is still preaching—the *heralding,* not the very Lord. Friedrich Heiler was rightly written: "Not speech *about* God, but speech *to* God, not the preaching of the revelation of God, but direct intercourse with God is, strictly speaking, the worship of God." When the rite is made central, prayer may become an incantation. When the book is made central, prayer may become an appendage of scribal interpretations. When preaching is made central, prayer...may become only an introduction and conclusion to the sermon. The heart of religion is in prayer—

the uplifting of human hands, the speaking of human lips, the expecting waiting of human silence—in direct communion with the Eternal. Prayer must go *through* the rite, scripture, symbolism, and sermon, as light through a window.

Then with what burden and awe the minister should prepare the prayers for public worship! Therein is the grievous failure, not to say disgrace, of Protestantism. "Brother So-and-so will lead us in prayer"; whereupon Brother So-and-so, in too many instances, offers God a slipshodness and a jumble, sometimes almost a brash irreverence, and has the temerity to call it prayer. Where public prayer is undisciplined, corporate public worship decays. There is a necessary preparation both of the pray-er and the prayer. What are its steps? The minister and the congregation should explore the wealth of prayers, "free" and liturgical, offered through the years. Wisdom was not born with us. There are collects of St. Chrysostom which are the perfect bloom of devotion. They cannot be touched without being spoiled. They can only be prayed, in gratitude for men who pray for us better than we pray for ourselves. Furthermore, prayers should spring from prior inquiry. What are the blessings for which we should praise God? What are the sins which should find corporate confession? What are the conflicts and sorrows that should be upborne in corporate intercession? As that last question is asked the compassionate minister will see the faces of his people and the tragic need of the world until intercession then and there interrupts his ponderings.

Then the minister must plan and write prayers as rigorously as sermons. The language should be wrought. God may be pleased with a clumsy prayer, but not when the clumsiness comes with sloth or a casual mind. The wording should not be "modern," despite the glib plea of the modern mind. Assuredly it should not be scientific or psychological. Every endeavor has right to its own idiom, providing the idiom is not a prison which the initiate cannot escape and the stranger cannot unlock. Religion is entitled to its own vocabulary—on the same terms. The idiom should be modern only in the sense that it does not rehearse ancient theological strife or outmoded ideas, or use coinage whose image and superscription is worn smooth. Otherwise prayer language should not be ancient or modern, but movingly human and plainly reverent—the language of a devotional poem.... Trite phrases—"Lord, bless all those we come in contact with"—and explosive phrases—"Lord, split our souls"—would be taboo; but quickening phrases, to give the mind its picture and the will its resolve, would be sought as treasure.

> THE COMPASSIONATE MINISTER WILL SEE THE FACES OF HIS PEOPLE AND THE TRAGIC NEED OF THE WORLD UNTIL INTERCESSION THEN AND THERE INTERRUPTS HIS PONDERINGS.

The planning of a prayer should be deliberate and clearly drawn. Later, in public utterance, the prayer may break its bounds to "take heaven by storm," but only if the bounds have first been set. How can petition or intercession be real unless it is specific and ordered? Prayer has its rapture like great music. Bach's *Toccata and Fugue in E Minor* breaks into a torrent of suns and stars. But the torrent has its reservoir, its gates opened and closed, and its appointed river bed. True rapture always knows prior disciplines....

The needs of the church are many and urgent. But they might all be met by the leaven of genuine corporate prayer. Only in God's light can the Church see light; only in His grace can the Church be redeemed—or redeem.

For biographical information on this author, see page 216.

The Priestly Expression of Prayer
WILLIAM H. WILLIMON — 2002

All of the church's work and worship could be construed as response to the Word read, heard, and proclaimed. Having listened to God, the church now joins in Christ's high priestly ministry and dares to speak to God in prayer. As is sometimes the custom to say as we begin to pray the Lord's Prayer, "We are bold to say, 'Our Father....'" Of course the pastor is not the only one in the church who may address God in prayer, but when the pastor prays, the pastor prays on behalf of, and at the authorization of, the whole church. The pastor's prayers, particularly in common worship on Sunday, ought to be clearly communal, informed by the prayers of the saints down through the ages, cognizant of all those concerns and needs felt throughout the church, not only in the congregation, but at all times and places.

Whereas prayer is the church's speech to God and not to the congregation, it is undeniable that the pastor teaches the congregation about prayer in the pastor's leadership of the Sunday prayers. Do our prayers ever reach beyond the confines of our congregation? Have we prayed for our enemies? Are our prayers only petition, or do they also include confession, praise, adoration, thanksgiving, and the full range of notes that we find in biblical prayer, such as in the psalter, the prayer book, and hymnbook of Israel? The pastor's ministry of public prayer will be based in great part on the pastor's own prayer life, the pastor's continual practice of the presence of God in prayer. In prayer, the pastor does most explicitly and publicly what a pastor does throughout the week—lift the congregation and its needs, the world and its needs, before the throne of God. Thus the pastor's leadership of prayer is a wonderfully formative aspect of the pastor's total ministry. Our pastoral leadership ought to have as its goal the enabling of the congregation to speak and to listen to God. Pastoral prayer on Sunday ought to be more like a hymn than a sermon. Note that Justin says, "We all stand up together and offer prayers."

WILLIAM H. WILLIMON is Dean of the Chapel and professor of Christian ministry at Duke University Divinity School and the author of numerous books, including *Calling and Character: Virtues of the Ordained Life* and *Sunday Dinner: The Lord's Supper and the Christian Life.*

Healing through P.A.I.N.
BRIAN J. DODD—1997

The Gospels are united on this testimony: Jesus went about healing and working wonders as he taught and preached. Everywhere Jesus went, the sick and infirm were brought to him for his healing touch. Epileptics, lepers, the lame and deaf and blind. Each time he healed, Jesus demonstrated his divine nature and the presence of the kingdom.

Jesus bestowed this same healing power on his disciples. To pray for healing is another way of praying for the coming of the kingdom. While he was still with them, he sent them out in pairs with the instructions, "cure the sick who are there, and say to them, 'The kingdom of God has come near to you'" (Lk. 10:9). After his crucifixion and resurrection, the healing works continued and confirmed the presence of the kingdom and the validity of the church as God's chosen vehicle. Jesus' words were fulfilled: "Very truly, I tell you, the one who believes in me will also do the works that I do and, in fact, will do greater works than these, because I am going to the Father" (Jn 14:12). Praying for healing is praying Jesus' way.

Some Christians believe that miraculous powers ended with the death of the first apostles, but most believe in praying for healing. There is a widespread belief inside and outside the church that prayer can help people recover from injury, illness and disease. According to a recent survey, 79 percent of Americans believe so, and 56 percent claim their faith has aided their recovery from sickness or injury. Hospitalization mobilizes the prayer chains: "Heal John's heart." "Use the surgeons to heal the blockage in Mary's stomach." "Heal our pastor's flu so he can preach on Sunday." "Heal the pain in Ruth's back and the tumor in Bill's brain."

Technique does not seem to matter greatly. Sometimes we lay on hands for healing as Jesus did. "Are any among you sick? They should call for the elders of the church and have them pray over them, anointing them with oil in the name of the Lord. The prayer of faith will save [heal] the sick, and the Lord will raise them up" (Jas 5:14–15). Other times we simply pray from where we are, and the healing power goes out (see Mk 5:25–34). Once Jesus used his saliva to make a mud balm, spreading it on a blind man's eyes and "saying to him, 'Go, wash in the pool of Siloam.'…Then he went and washed and came back able to see" (Jn 9:6–7). The presence of the kingdom is demonstrated as God hears people's cries and responds to them with a healing touch.

Jesus did not heal everybody. There were crowds that he walked past, and there were people he did not deliver. There is no evidence that Jesus' prayers for healing ever failed, but the disciples experienced the frustration of unanswered prayer. Once they prayed for a boy who was unable to speak and had seizures. The father of that boy bluntly said to Jesus, "I asked your disciples to cast it out, but they could not do so" (Mk 9:18). Frankly, I find great encouragement in knowing that the disciples, like me, experienced the frustration of unanswered prayer.

There are various explanations for why some prayers go unanswered: unconfessed sin, undetected doubt, unyielded pray-er, and so on. But all we really know is that some of our prayers are not answered as we ask them. We pray for healing, but the cancer runs its course and kills its victim. We may rationalize that the deceased actually was healed, that is, received the ultimate healing transformation that comes with entering eternal life. This is true, but it does not change the fact that we did not receive the healing that we prayed for.

Jesus has already prepared us for unanswered prayer with his experience in the garden of Gethsemane where he prayed, "Let this cup pass from me." He was yielded to God's purpose even as he asked this, so he continued, "yet not what I want but what you want" (Mt 26:39). Again the Lord's Prayer serves as our guide to prayer. We pray "your will be done," submitting our desires to God's purposes. We ask sincerely, but then we yield ourselves to the wisdom and mercy of God, confident "that all things work together for good for those who love God, who are called according to his purpose" (Rom 8:28).

Those who suffer from chronic or acute pain can take some cues from how Jesus prayed through his pain as he faced the agony of the cross in the garden of Gethsemane. He prayed to avoid temptation, he involved others in praying with him, and he yielded himself up with "not my will but yours be done" (Lk. 22:40–46 par. Mt 26:36–44 and Mk 14:32–39). These four aspects of Jesus' prayer form an acronym that reminds us how to pray through pain (P.A.I.N.):

Pray.

Avoid temptation.

Involve others.

Not my will but God's be done.

Acute or chronic pain challenges our faith more than anything. We are tempted to cry out, "Why?" and "Where are you, God?" God always reveals himself eventually, but the peace that accompanies prayer can bring great comfort and relief to us in our painful struggle.

For biographical information on this author, see page 178.

The Laying on of Hands
RICHARD FOSTER—*1992*

[The laying on of hands] is a teaching found throughout the Bible, and it is a valid ministry ordained by God for the benefit of the community of faith. It is not an empty ritual but a clear understanding of the law of contact and transmittal. It is one means through which God imparts to us what we desire or need, or what God in his infinite wisdom knows is best for us. It is one of the elementary matters of the Gospel without which we cannot go on to maturity (Heb. 6:1–6).

The laying on of hands is used in Scripture in a number of ways such as the tribal blessing, the baptism in the Holy Spirit, and the impartation of spiritual gifts, but one of its most pre-eminent uses is in Healing Prayer. Jesus laid hands on the sick at Nazareth and healed them (Mark 6:5). He laid his hands on the blind man at Bethsaida twice before he fully recovered his sight (Mark 8:22–25). On the island of Malta the Apostle Paul laid hands on the sick, and they were healed (Acts 28:7–10). In the longer ending of Mark's Gospel ordinary believers are encouraged in this ministry (Mark 16:18).

The laying on of hands in itself does not heal the sick—it is Christ who heals the sick. The laying on of hands is a simple act of obedience that quickens our faith and gives God the opportunity to impart healing. Often people will add the accompanying means of anointing with oil, following the counsel of James 5:14. Like many others I have discovered that, when praying for people with the laying on of hands, I sometimes detect a gentle flow of energy. I have found that I cannot make the flow of heavenly life happen, but I can stop it. If I resist or refuse to be an open conduit for God's power to come into a person, it will stop. Also, a spirit of hate or resentment arrests the flow of life immediately. Unforgiveness on the part of the person receiving ministry is also a roadblock.

Obviously, common sense and a respect for the integrity of others will keep us from engaging in this work lightly or carelessly. We simply do not go around plopping our hands on anyone we please. Paul cautions about laying hands on people indiscriminately because it might bring them into things for which they are not ready (1 Tim. 5:22). Sanctified common sense will teach us what is appropriate at any given time.

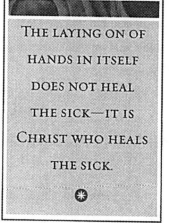

THE LAYING ON OF HANDS IN ITSELF DOES NOT HEAL THE SICK—IT IS CHRIST WHO HEALS THE SICK.

I might add that while we adults struggle with this idea of the laying on of hands, children have no difficulty with it. I was once called to a home to pray for a seriously ill baby. Her four-year-old brother was in the room, and so I told him I needed his help in praying for his baby sister. He was delighted to help, and I was delighted to have him, for I know that children can often pray with unusual effectiveness. He climbed up into the chair beside me. "Let's play a little game," I suggested. "Since we know that Jesus is always with us, let's suppose that he is sitting over in that chair across from us. He is waiting patiently for us to focus our attention on him. When we see him and the love in his eyes, we start thinking more about his love than about how sick Julie is. He smiles, gets up, and comes over to us. When that happens, we both put our hands on Julie, and as we do, Jesus puts his hands right on top of ours. He releases his healing light right into your little sister sort of like a whole bunch of soldiers who go in and fight the bad germs until they are all gone. Okay?" Seriously the boy nodded. Together we prayed just as I had described it to him, and then we thanked God that this was the way it was going to be. Amen. While we prayed, I sensed that my small prayer partner had exercised unusual faith.

The next morning Julie was perfectly well. Now, I cannot prove to you that our little prayer game made Julie well. All I know is that Julie was healed, and that was all I needed to know.

For biographical information on this author, see page 19.

Anointing with Oil in the Name of the Lord
ANDREW MURRAY — 1934

Is any one of you sick? He should call the elders of the church to pray over him and anoint him with oil in the name of the Lord (James 5:14).

There has been some controversy over James's instructions to anoint the sick person with oil in the name of the Lord. Some have inferred that apart from prescribing the prayer of faith alone, without the use of remedies, James had, on the contrary, mentioned anointing with oil as a remedy to be employed, and that to anoint in the name of the Lord had no other meaning than to rub the patient with oil. But since this prescription applies to all kinds of sickness, this interpretation would attribute to oil a miraculous virtue against every kind of illness. Let's look at what the Scripture says about anointing with oil and what sense it attaches to these two words.

It was the custom of the people in the East to anoint themselves with oil when they came out of the bath, a most refreshing practice in a hot climate. We see also that all those who were called to the special service of God were to be anointed with oil as a token of their consecration to God and of the grace they should receive from Him to fulfill their vocation. The oil that was used to anoint the priests and the tabernacle was looked upon as "most holy" (Exodus 30:22–32), and wherever the Bible speaks of anointing with oil, it is a symbol of holiness and consecration. Nowhere in the Bible do we find any proof that oil was used as a remedy.

In Mark 6:13, we read that the twelve "drove out many demons and anointed many sick people with oil and healed them." Here the healing of the sick runs parallel with the casting out of demons: both the result of miraculous power. Such was the kind of mission that Jesus commanded His disciples when He sent them out two by two: "He...gave them authority to drive out evil spirits and to heal every disease and sickness"

(Matthew 10:1). So it was the same power that permitted them either to cast out evil spirits or to heal the sick.

What was symbolized by the anointing administered by the twelve? In the Old Testament, oil was the symbol of the gift of the Holy Spirit: "The Spirit of the Lord God is upon me; because the Lord hath anointed me" (Isaiah 61:1). It is said of the Lord Jesus in the New Testament, "God anointed Jesus of Nazareth with the Holy Spirit and power, and…he went around doing good and healing all who were under the power of the devil, because God was with him" (Acts 10:38). It is said of believers, "You have an anointing from the Holy One, and all of you know the truth" (1 John 2:20). Sometimes man feels the need of a visible sign, appealing to his senses, which may help to sustain his faith and enable him to grasp the spiritual meaning. The anointing, therefore, should symbolize to the sick the action of the Holy Spirit, who gives the healing.

Do we then need the anointing as well the prayer of faith? It is the Word of God that prescribes it, and it is in order to follow its teachings that most of those who pray for healing receive the anointing; not that they regard it as indispensable, but to show that they are ready to submit to the Word of God in all things. In the last promise made by the Lord Jesus, He ordains the laying on of hands, not the anointing, to accompany the communication of healing virtue (Mark 16:18). When Paul circumcised Timothy and took upon himself a special vow, it was to prove that he had no objection to observing the institutions of the old covenant as long as the liberty of the gospel did not suffer. In the same way, James, the head of the church of Jerusalem, faithful in preserving as far as possible the institutions of his fathers, continued the system of the Holy Spirit. We also should regard it not as a remedy but as a pledge of the mighty virtue of the Holy Spirit, as a means of strengthening faith, a point of contact and of communion between the sick and the members of the church who are called to anoint him with oil.

For biographical information on this author, see page 14.

The Four Basic Kinds of Healing
FRANCIS MACNUTT—1974

There are four different kinds of basic healing differentiated by the kinds of sickness that afflict us and the basic causes of those sicknesses. Unless we know these differences, we will not be able to help most people. In fact, we may harm them by insisting on one particular diagnosis and one particular method of prayer when a different diagnosis and a different type of treatment and prayer are needed. Someone, for instance, who has had experience only with deliverance and exorcism—who has no knowledge or experience of the value of psychological healing ("healing of the memories")—can do untold damage by insisting on casting out devils every time he tries to help a person who has a psychological problem. Some psychological problems seem to be caused by demonic infestation but most problems in my experience can be explained by the natural causality of past hurts and rejections in a person's life. Still other psychological problems are caused by such physical causes as chemical and enzyme imbalances in the bloodstream (e.g., postpartum depression).

So anyone who hopes to pray for the sick should realize that there are three basic kinds of sickness, each requiring a different kind of prayer:

1) Sickness of our spirit, caused by our own personal sin.

2) Emotional sickness and problems (e.g., anxiety) caused by the emotional hurts of our past.

3) Physical sickness in our bodies, caused by disease or accidents.

In addition, any of the above—sin, emotional problems or physical sickness—can be caused by demonic oppression, a different cause that requires a different prayer approach, namely, prayer for exorcism.

Consequently, there are at least *four basic prayer methods* we must understand in order to exercise a complete healing ministry:

1) prayer for *repentance* (for personal sin),

2) prayer for *inner healing* ("healing of memories") (for emotional problems),

3) prayer for *physical healing* (for physical sickness),

4) prayer for *deliverance* (exorcism) (for demonic oppression).

Not all of us will have a deep ministry in each of these areas, but we should know our own limitations and be ready to refer a person to someone else who has more experience than we in one or the other area. I look forward to a time when Christians in every locality will be able to join their gifts to work as a team, much as doctors work together in any hospital or clinic. Most of us don't have the time or God-given gifts to work in all these areas of healing. But each of us needs to develop the discernment to judge what is wrong and the appropriate type of prayer to use.

This becomes even more important when we meet people who seem to need *all* these forms of prayer. For example, a middle-aged woman may ask for prayer to be cured of arthritis (physical healing); upon talking to her you find she was deeply hurt by her father when she was young (inner healing), and that she was never able to forgive him (repentance); nor has she been able as a woman to relate to her husband (inner healing probably); in her search for a way out of her predicament she has attended séances where she has supposedly met a "spirit-guide" from the dead who gives her guidance through automatic writing (a need for deliverance is here indicated)....

Ordinarily, of course, God works through doctors, psychiatrists, counselors and nurses to facilitate nature's healing process. This may seem so obvious as to go without saying, except that there are some evangelists who set up an artificial opposition between prayer and medicine—as if God's way of healing is through prayer, while the medical profession is a secular means of healing, somehow unworthy of Christians who have real faith. Consequently, they encourage people to pray and not to see their doctor. But God works through the doctor to heal as well as through the prayer for healing—the doctor, the counselor and the nurse are all ministers of healing. All these different professions, with their different competencies, go to make up God's healing team. Any time we disparage any person who helps bring about the healing of the whole man we are destroying the kind of cooperative healing ministry that the Christian community might have and are setting up false divisions between divine and human healing methods.

FRANCIS MACNUTT is known around the world for his preaching and healing ministry. His numerous books include *Prayer That Heals*, *Overcome by the Spirit*, and *Deliverance from Evil Spirits*.

Spiritual Direction
EMILIE GRIFFIN — 2001

The ancient discipline of spiritual direction, once confined to religious communities, is now used broadly by lay people as well. Meetings with a trained director, weekly, monthly, or at longer intervals, may help us to sustain a regular commitment to prayer. In the meetings we describe our prayer experiences, our joys and difficulties, and gain perspective on how prayer may be shaping us. The spiritual director helps us to develop confidence in God, to relax in prayer, to deal with the trouble spots of any kind. Spiritual direction is not entirely professionalized, but there are now many trained directors. The director should be a person experienced in prayer and able to listen.

Spiritual direction can become a deeply valued aspect of our prayer lives. Sometimes these relationships take on the character of friendships. However, as long as the direction is in progress, maintaining a certain holy distance is good. Keep confidentiality, both for your sake and the director's. As with retreats, spiritual direction is a work of the Holy Spirit. Honor and treasure it as such.

For biographical information on this author, see page 146.

PRAYER

"Have faith in God," Jesus answered. "I tell you the truth, if anyone says to this mountain, 'Go, throw yourself into the sea,' and does not doubt in his heart but believes that what he says will happen, it will be done for him. Therefore I tell you, whatever you ask for in prayer, believe that you have received it, and it will be yours. And when you stand praying, if you hold anything against anyone, forgive him, so that your Father in heaven may forgive you your sins."

MARK 11:22–25

CHAPTER 10

THE
POWER
OF
PRAYER

❖

The Key of the Greater Work
OSWALD CHAMBERS—1910s

"I say to you, he who believes in Me,...greater works than these he will do, because I go to My Father" (John 14:12).

Prayer does not equip us for greater works—prayer *is* the greater work. Yet we think of prayer as some commonsense exercise of our higher powers that simply prepares us for God's work. In the teachings of Jesus Christ, prayer is the working of the miracle of redemption in me, which produces the miracle of redemption in others through the power of God. The way fruit remains firm is through prayer, but remember that it is prayer based on the agony of Christ in redemption, not on my own agony. We must go to God as His child, because only a child gets his prayers answered; a "wise" man does not (see Matthew 11:25).

Prayer is *the* battle, and it makes no difference where you are. However God may engineer your circumstances, your duty is to pray. Never allow yourself this thought, "I am of no use where I am," because you certainly cannot be used where you have not yet been placed. Wherever God has placed you and

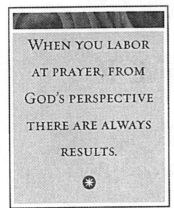

WHEN YOU LABOR AT PRAYER, FROM GOD'S PERSPECTIVE THERE ARE ALWAYS RESULTS.

whatever your circumstances, you should pray, continually offering up prayers to Him. And He promises, "Whatever you ask in My name, that I will do..." (14:13). Yet we refuse to pray unless it thrills or excites us, which is the most intense form of spiritual selfishness. We must learn to work according to God's direction, and He says to *pray.* "Pray the Lord of the harvest to send out laborers into His harvest" (Matthew 9:38).

There is nothing thrilling about a laboring person's work, but it is the laboring person who makes the ideas of the genius possible. And it is the laboring saint who makes the ideas of his Master possible. When you labor at prayer, from God's perspective there are always results. What an astonishment it will be to see, once the veil is finally lifted, all the souls that have been reaped by you, simply because you have been in the habit of taking your orders from Jesus Christ.

OSWALD CHAMBERS (1874–1917) is best known for his book *My Utmost for His Highest,* (first published by his wife in 1928), which has become one of the most popular devotional books of all time. His other works include *If You Will Ask: Reflections on the Power of Prayer* and *The Love of God.* Biography: *Oswald Chambers: Abandoned to God—The Life Story of the author of My Utmost for His Highest.*

The Source of Power

S. D. GORDON — 1904

There is one inlet of power in life—anybody's life—any kind of power: just one inlet—the Holy Spirit. He is power. He is in every one who opens his door to God. He eagerly enters every open door. He comes in by our invitation and consent. His presence within is the vital thing.

But with many of us while He is in, He is not in control: in as guest; not as host. That is to say He is hindered in His natural movements; tied up, so that He cannot do what He would. And so we are not conscious or only partially conscious of His presence. And others are still less so. But to yield to His [the Holy Spirit's] mastery, to cultivate His friendship, to give Him full swing—that will result in what is called power. One inlet of power—the Holy Spirit in control.

S. D. GORDON (1859–1936), born in Philadelphia, was a well-known devotional writer whose twenty or so books were read widely in the early years of the twentieth century. He worked for many years with the YMCA and other parachurch organizations. His best-known books include *Quiet Talks on Power, Quiet Talks on Prayer,* and *Quiet Talks on Jesus.*

The Power of Earnest Prayer
Jonathan Edwards — 1740

Most of the remarkable deliverances and restorations of the church of God, that we have account of in the Scripture, were in answer to prayer. So was the redemption of the church of God from the Egyptian bondage (Ex. 2:23 and 3:7). The great restoration of the church in the latter day, is often spoken of as resembled by this; as in Is. 64:1–4, 11:11, 15–16, 43:2–3, 16–19, 51:10–11, 15, 63:11–13; Zech. 10:10–11; Hos. 2:14–15. It was in answer to prayer, that the sun stood still over Gibeon, and the moon in the valley of Aijalon (Josh. 10:12), and God's people obtained that great victory over their enemies: in which wonderful miracle, God seemed to have some respect to a future more glorious event to be accomplished for the Christian church, in the day of her victory over her enemies, in the latter days; even that event foretold Is. 60:20. "Thy sun shall no more go down, neither shall thy moon withdraw itself." It was in answer to prayer, that God delivered his church from the mighty host of the Assyrians, in Hezekiah's time; which dispensation is abundantly made use of, as a type of the great things God will do for the Christian church in the latter days, in the prophecies of Isaiah.

The restoration of the church of God from the Babylonish captivity, as abundantly appears both by scripture prophecies and histories, was in answer to extraordinary prayer; see Jer. 29:10–14, and 50:4–5; Dan. 9 throughout; Ezra 8:21 ff.; Neh.

1:4–11, 4:4–5, and chapter 9 throughout. This restoration of the Jewish church, after the destruction of Babylon, is evidently a type of the glorious restoration of the Christian church, after the destruction of the kingdom of Antichrist; which (as all know) is abundantly spoken of in the Revelation of St. John, as the antitype of Babylon. Samson, out of weakness, received strength to pull down Dagon's temple, through prayer [Judg. 16:28–30]. So the people of God, in the latter days, will out of weakness be made strong, and will become the instruments of pulling down the kingdom of Satan, by prayer.

The Spirit of God was poured out upon Christ himself, in answer to prayer (Luke 3:21–22). "Now when all the people were baptized, it came to pass, that Jesus also being baptized, and praying, the heaven was opened, and the Holy Ghost descended in a bodily shape like a dove, upon him; and a voice came from heaven, which said, Thou art my beloved Son, in thee I am well pleased." The Spirit descends on the church of Christ, the same way, in this respect, that it descended on the head of the church. The greatest effusion of the Spirit that ever yet has been, even that which was in the primitive times of the Christian church, which began in Jerusalem on the day of Pentecost, was in answer to extraordinary prayer. When the disciples were gathered together to their Lord, a little before his ascension, "he commanded them that they should not depart from Jerusalem, but wait for the promise of the Father, which" (saith he) "ye have heard of me," i.e., the promise of the Holy

Ghost (Acts 1:4). What they had their hearts upon was the restoration of the kingdom to Israel: "Lord," (say they) "wilt thou, at this time, restore again the kingdom to Israel" (v.6)? And according to Christ's direction after his ascension, they returned to Jerusalem, and continued in united fervent prayer and supplication. It seems they spent their time in it from day to day, without ceasing; till the Spirit came down in a wonderful manner upon them, and that work was begun which never ceased, till the world was turned upside down, and all the chief nations of it were converted to Christianity....

> IN THAT GREAT OUT-POURING OF THE SPIRIT THAT WAS IN THE DAYS OF THE APOSTLES, THE SPIRIT CAME DOWN FIRST ON THOSE THAT WERE ENGAGED IN UNITED EARNEST PRAYER FOR IT.
>
> ✺

As there is so great and manifold reason from the Word of God, to think that if a spirit of earnest prayer for that great effusion of the Spirit of God which I am speaking of, prevailed in the Christian church, the mercy would be soon granted; so those that are engaged in such prayer might expect the first benefit. God will come to those that are seeking him and waiting for him (Is. 25:9 and 26:8). When Christ came in flesh, he was first revealed to them who were "waiting for the consolation of Israel," and "looking for redemption in Jerusalem" (Luke 2:25, 38). And in that great outpouring of the Spirit that was in the days of the apostles, which was attended with such glorious effects among Jews and Gentiles, the Spirit came down first on those that were engaged in united earnest prayer for it (Acts 1:14). A special blessing is promised to them that love and pray for the prosperity of the church of God (Ps. 122:6). "Pray for the peace of Jerusalem. They shall prosper, that love thee."

For biographical information on this author, see page 100.

The Power of Praying Together
CHARLES H. SPURGEON — 1885

As many mercies are transported from heaven in the ship of prayer, so *there are many special mercies that can only be brought to us by the fleets of united prayer.* Many are the good things that God will give to his lonely Elijahs and Daniels, but if two of you agree as touching anything that you ask, there is no limit to God's bountiful answers (Matt. 18:19).

Peter may have never been brought out of prison had it not been that prayer was made without ceasing by all the church for him (Acts 12:5). Pentecost might never have come had not *all* the disciples been with one accord in one place (Acts 2:1), waiting for the descent of the tongues of fire. God is pleased to answer individual prayers, but at times He seems to say, You may entreat My favor, but I will not see your face unless your brethren are with you. Why is this? I take it that our gracious Lord is setting forth His own esteem for the communion of saints. "I believe in the communion of saints" is one article of the great Christian creed, but how few saints understand it. And yet there is such a thing as real union among God's people.

We cannot afford to lose the help and love of our brethren. Augustine says, "The poor are made for the rich, and the rich are made for the poor." I do not doubt but the strong saints are made for the weak saints and the weak saints bring special benedictions upon mature believers. There is a completeness in the whole body of Christ—each joint owes something to every other joint, and "the whole body is bound together by that which every joint supplies...."

The value placed upon union and communion among the people of God is seen by the fact that there are certain mercies that are bestowed only when the saints pray unitedly. How we ought to feel this bond of union! How we ought to pray for one another!

CHARLES H. SPURGEON (1834–1892) was a Baptist preacher and founding pastor of the Metropolitan Tabernacle in London and became known as "the prince of preachers" in the nineteenth century. His collected sermons filled more than fifty volumes.

The Power of a Timid Prayer
MAX LUCADO — 1993

Some of you pray like a Concorde jet—smooth, sleek, high, and mighty. Your words reverberate in the clouds and send sonic booms throughout the heavens. If you pray like a Concorde, I salute you. If you don't, I understand.

Maybe you are like me, more a crop duster than a Concorde. You aren't flashy, you fly low, you seem to cover the same ground a lot, and some mornings it's tough to get the old engine cranked up.

Most of us are like that. Most of our prayer lives could use a tune-up.

Some prayer lives lack consistency. They're either a desert or an oasis. Long, arid, dry spells interrupted by brief plunges into the waters of communion. We go days or weeks without consistent prayer, but then something happens—we hear a sermon, read a book, experience a tragedy—something leads us to pray, so we dive in. We submerge ourselves in prayer and leave refreshed and renewed. But as the journey resumes, our prayers don't.

Others of us need sincerity. Our prayers are a bit hollow, memorized, and rigid. More liturgy than life. And though they are daily, they are dull.

Still others lack, well, honesty. We honestly wonder if prayer makes a difference. Why on earth would God in heaven want to talk to me? If God knows all, who am I to tell him anything? If God controls all, who am I to do anything?

If you struggle with prayer, I've got just the guy for you. Don't worry, he's not a monastic saint. He's not a calloused-kneed apostle. Nor is he a prophet whose middle name is

Meditation. He's not a too-holy-to-be-you reminder of how far you need to go in prayer. He's just the opposite. A fellow crop duster. A parent with a sick son in need of a miracle. The father's

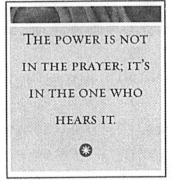

THE POWER IS NOT IN THE PRAYER; IT'S IN THE ONE WHO HEARS IT.

prayer isn't much, but the answer is and the result reminds us: The power is not in the prayer; it's in the one who hears it.

He prays out of desperation. His son, his only son, was demon-possessed. Not only was he a deaf mute and an epileptic, he was also possessed by an evil spirit. Ever since the boy was young, the demon had thrown him into fires and water.

Imagine the pain of the father. Other dads could watch their children grow and mature; he could only watch his suffer. While others were teaching their sons an occupation, he was just trying to keep his son alive.

What a challenge! He couldn't leave his son alone for a minute. Who knew when the next attack would come? The father had to remain on call, on alert twenty-four hours a day. He was desperate and tired, and his prayer reflects both.

"If you can do anything for him, please have pity on us and help us."

Listen to that prayer. Does it sound courageous? Confident? Strong? Hardly.

One word would have made a lot of difference. Instead of

if, what if he'd said *since?* "*Since* you can do anything for him, please have pity on us and help us."

But that's not what he said. He said *if.* The Greek is even more emphatic. The tense implies doubt. It's as if the man were saying, "This one's probably out of your league, but if you can…"

A classic crop-duster appeal. More meek than mighty. More timid than towering. More like a crippled lamb coming to a shepherd than a proud lion roaring in the jungle. If his prayer sounds like yours, then don't be discouraged, for that's where prayer begins. It begins as a yearning. An honest appeal. Ordinary people staring at Mount Everest. No pretense. No boasting. No posturing. Just prayer. Feeble prayer, but prayer nonetheless.

We are tempted to wait to pray until we know how to pray. We've heard the prayers of the spiritually mature. We've read of the rigors of the disciplined. And we are convinced we've a long way to traverse.

And since we'd rather not pray than pray poorly, we don't pray. Or we pray infrequently. We are waiting to pray until we learn how to pray.

Good thing this man didn't make the same mistake. He wasn't much of a pray-er. And his wasn't much of a prayer. He even admits it! "I do believe," he implored. "Help me to believe more" (see Mark 9:24).

This prayer isn't destined for a worship manual. No Psalm will result from his utterance.…But Jesus responded. He responded, not to the eloquence of the man, but to the pain of the man.…

Look at the chaos that greets him....The disciples and the religious leaders are arguing. A crowd of bystanders is gawking. A boy, who'd suffered all his life, is on public display. And a father who'd come for help is despondent, wondering why no one can help.

No wonder Jesus says, "You people have no faith. How long must I stay with you? How long must I put up with you?" (v. 19).

Never has the difference between heaven and earth been so stark.

Never has the arena of prayer been so poor. Where is the faith in this picture? The disciples have failed, the scribes are amused, the demon is victorious, and the father is desperate. You'd be hard-pressed to find a needle of belief in that haystack....

And yet out of the din of doubt comes your timid voice. "If you can do anything for me…"

Does such a prayer make a difference?

Let Mark answer that question.

When Jesus saw that a crowd was quickly gathering, he ordered the evil spirit, saying, "You spirit that makes people unable to hear or speak, I command you to come out of this boy and never enter him again."

The evil spirit screamed and caused the boy to fall on the ground again. Then the spirit came out. The boy looked as if he were dead, and many people said, "He is dead!" But Jesus took hold of the boy's hand and helped him to stand up. (Mark 9:25–27)

This troubled the disciples. As soon as they got away from the crowds they asked Jesus, "Why couldn't we force that evil spirit out?"

His answer? "That kind of spirit can only be forced out by prayer."

What prayer? What prayer made the difference? Was it the prayer of the apostles? No, they didn't pray. Must have been the prayers of the scribes. Maybe they went to the temple and interceded. No. The scribes didn't pray either. Then it must have been the people. Perhaps they had a vigil for the boy. Nope. The people didn't pray. They never bent a knee. Then what prayer led Jesus to deliver the demon?

There is only one prayer in the story. It's the honest prayer of a hurting man. And since God is more moved by our hurt than our eloquence, he responded. That's what fathers do.

MAX LUCADO is the author of many best-selling books, including *In the Grip of Grace, The Great House of God,* and *No Wonder They Call Him the Savior.* He was a missionary to Brazil and presently preaches for the Oak Hills Church of Christ in San Antonio, Texas, where he lives with his wife and children.

Prayer As Public Good
EUGENE H. PETERSON — *1985*

Prayer is political action. Prayer is social energy. Prayer is public good. Far more of our nation's life is shaped by prayer than is formed by legislation. That we have not collapsed into anarchy is due more to prayer than to the police. Prayer is a sustained and intricate act of patriotism in the largest sense of that word—far more precise and loving and preserving than any patriotism served up in slogans. That society continues to be livable and that hope continues to be resurgent are attributable to prayer far more than to business prosperity or a flourishing of the arts. The single most important action contributing to whatever health and strength there is in our land is prayer.

For biographical information on this author, see page 56.

God's Day of Power
E. M. Bounds — 1895

The more praying there is in the world the better the world will be, the mightier the forces against evil everywhere. Prayer, in one phase of its operation, is a disinfectant and a preventive. It purifies the air; it destroys the contagion of evil. Prayer is not a fitful, shortlived thing. It is no voice crying unheard and unheeded in the silence. It is a voice which goes into God's ear, and it lives as long as God's ear is open to holy pleas, as long as God's heart is alive to holy things.

God shapes the world by prayer. Prayers are deathless. The lips that uttered the prayers may be closed in death, the heart that felt them may be closed in death, the heart that felt them may have ceased to beat, but the prayers live before God, and God's heart is set on them and prayers outlive the lives of those who uttered them; outlive a generation, outlive an age, outlive a world.

That man is the most immortal who has done the most and the best praying. They are God's vice-regents. A man can pray better because of the prayers of the past; a man can live holier because of the prayers of the past; the man of many and acceptable prayers has done the truest and greatest service to the incoming generation. The prayers of God's saints strengthen the unborn generation against the desolating waves of sin and evil. Woe to the generation of sons who find their censers empty of the rich incense of prayer; whose fathers have been too busy or too unbelieving to pray, and perils inexpressible and consequences untold are their unhappy heritage. Fortunate are they whose fathers and mothers have left them a wealthy patrimony of prayer.

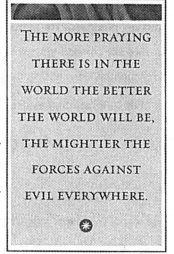

THE MORE PRAYING THERE IS IN THE WORLD THE BETTER THE WORLD WILL BE, THE MIGHTIER THE FORCES AGAINST EVIL EVERYWHERE.

The prayers of God's saints are the capital stock in heaven by which Christ carries on His great work upon earth. The great throes and mighty convulsions on earth are the results of these prayers. Earth is changed, revolutionized, angels move on more powerful, more rapid wing, and God's policy is shaped as the prayers are more numerous, more efficient.

It is true that the mightiest successes that come to God's cause are created and carried on by prayer. God's day of power; the angelic days of activity and power are when God's Church comes into its mightiest inheritance of mightiest faith and mightiest prayer. God's conquering days are when the saints have given themselves to mightiest prayer. When God's house on earth is a house of prayer, then God's house in heaven is busy and all potent in its plans and movements, then His earthly armies are clothed with the triumphs and spoils of victory and His enemies defeated on every hand.

For biographical information on this author, see page 119.

Putting God on the Spot
Tony Evans — *1998*

I am often asked the question, "If God is going to do what He wants to do anyway, why do I need to pray?"

Answer: Because Scripture tells us that there are certain things God will not do apart from our prayers.

Don't ask me to explain why God chose to do things this way. I just know that He did.

We do somewhat the same thing with our children. We want them to ask us for things that they need, because asking teaches them dependence. It teaches them that the good things of life don't just materialize out of thin air, but are provided by someone who loves them. Asking also teaches our children gratitude, because they need to learn to say "Thank you" when they receive something. And asking gives our kids access to the good things we have for them.

One of the best examples of a believer approaching God in prayer is the prayer of the prophet Daniel (Daniel 9:1–19)....Daniel knew from his knowledge of Jeremiah's prophecy (v. 2) that the seventy years of Israel's captivity were about to end.

So Daniel proceeded to pray a great prayer in which he confessed his people's sin and called on God to remember His covenant with Israel and end His people's humiliation in exile from Jerusalem.

In other words, Daniel prayed God's own Word back to Him and called on Him to honor it.

One of the great things about prayer, especially if you know the Word of God, is that in prayer you can hold God to His Word. I don't mean you can coerce Him, but you can pray like Daniel, "O Lord, hear! O Lord, forgive! O Lord, listen and take action! For Thine own sake, O my God, do not delay, because Thy city and Thy people are called by Thy name" (v. 19).

Daniel was reminding God of what He had said about Jerusalem and its people. He was holding God to His Word. Moses did the same thing when God announced He wanted to destroy Israel and start over with Moses (Exodus 32:10).

Moses went before the Lord and reminded Him of three things (vv. 11–13). He reminded God that these were the people He had rescued from Egypt. Moses reminded God that if He destroyed the nation, the Egyptians would accuse God of doing evil.

And finally, Moses reminded God of His great promises to Abraham and his descendants. Then verse 14 says, "The Lord changed His mind." God was still sovereign in this situation, but from our human standpoint the intercession of Moses caused God to change His plans.

Moses knew how to pray. He basically said, "God, if You do this, Your name is going to look bad, and You will be embarrassed among the gods. God, it is in Your best interest to preserve Your people. You need to forgive Your people."

I call this putting God on the spot. Moses was able to do this in his prayer because he understood God's nature. Moses appealed to God's grace, knowing that His grace could overrule His wrath.

But Moses had to pray before God would relent. In His sovereignty, God decided that He would allow Moses' prayer to "change His mind."

We have the same privilege as Moses to hold God to His Word in prayer. It's not a matter of His reluctance to fulfill His Word, but a test of our faith to believe and act on His Word.

TONY EVANS is pastor of Oak Cliff Fellowship in Dallas, Texas, and president of the Urban Alternative, a teaching ministry targeting the inner city. He is the author of numerous books, including *Returning to Your First Love* and *The Battle Is the Lord's.*

What God Wants Most
TIM STAFFORD — 1986

Prayer begins with communion, but it does not stop there. The New Testament encourages us to think of prayer as an opportunity to ask for help. We are told to request what we need. We are told that "we have not because we ask not" and that "prayer changes things." God does not depend on our requests to do the good he intends, nor can prayer make him do what he does not care to do. Yet the biblical teaching is unmistakable. He acts in response to our requests.

Again the question surfaces: Why does he want me to ask, since he already knows what I need? If I pray, like Jesus, "Let your will be done," am I not saying that I want God to do what he planned to do in the first place? Then why bother to ask him? Can it really be possible to change God's will? Does prayer have any power to affect events?

Another human analogy may illuminate this situation. Suppose a friend plans to change jobs. His direction is clear; he is sure it is the right move. He has only to act. So will he discuss it with me? Yes, often he will, though not because he wants my advice. He already knows the choice he should make, and I probably know very little about his profession. He discusses it because he wants my company; he wants my support, my agreement, before he acts.

God has chosen to root his power in our shared concerns, to act in communion with us. He does not *need* our consent to act—he *prefers* it. Put simply, he waits to act until he has talked it over with us. And he rarely takes the initiative. He waits until it matters enough to us to bring it up with him.

Stated that way, prayer is a startling responsibility. It is not just our own personal welfare that depends on it. It is the welfare of the world. Why would God choose to depend on us? Why wait for fickle attention to focus on the thing that needs doing? We find this difficult to understand because power is our first priority. We are worried about things getting done. He has no lack of power. He is the highest power in the universe. He makes his power subservient to our fickle attention because he is working toward the reconciliation of the world in love. When at long last we come to him with our concerns, we take the first small step toward what he wants most: communion.

God's decision to wait for our prayers is his second humiliation to the flesh. In the first he stripped off his glory and became a man to destroy the forces keeping man and God apart. Now he holds his power in check and waits for us to come. Reconciliation to us is his first priority. Just as on earth he chose to live within and act from the limitations of human flesh and blood, so now he chooses to do the same from the limitations of our concerns.

Why he cares so much for our company or precisely how our prayers affect his course, we may not understand. But Scripture leaves no doubt that in prayer we have the tremendous privilege of participation in his power. To grow stronger in prayer I need not work myself into a mental state that denies probability, or find a praying technique that produces magical results. Growing stronger in prayer must mean growing stronger in an intimate, loving union with God, for he is the source of all power.

TIM STAFFORD, an award-winning author, is a regular contributor to *Christianity Today* and *Campus Life* magazines, author of *Knowing the Face of God,* and coeditor of *The Student Bible.*

The Laborers of Force
G. CAMPBELL MORGAN — 1906

There are saints of God who for long, long years have been shut off from all the activities of the Church, and even from the worship of the sanctuary, but who, nevertheless, have continued to labour together in prayer with the whole fellowship of the saints. There comes to me the thought of one woman who, to my knowledge, since 1872 in this great babel of

London, has been in perpetual pain, and yet in constant prayer. She is to-day a woman twisted and distorted by suffering, and yet exhaling the calm and strength of the secret of the Most High. In 1872 she was a bed-ridden girl in the North of London, praying that God would send revival to the Church of which she was a member, and yet into which even then she never came. She had read in the little paper called *Revival*...the story of a work being done in Chicago among ragged children by a man called Moody. She had never seen Moody, but putting that little paper under her pillow, she began to pray, "O Lord, send this man to our Church." She had no means of reaching him or communicating with him.

He had already visited the country in 1867, and in 1872 he started again for a short trip with no intention of doing any work. Mr. Lessey, however, the pastor of the church of which this girl was member, met him and asked him to preach for him. He consented, and after the evening service he asked those who would decide for Christ to rise, and hundreds did so. He was surprised, and imagined that his request had been misunderstood. He repeated it more clearly, and again the response was the same. Meetings were continued throughout the following ten days, and four hundred members were taken into the church. In telling me this story Moody said, "I wanted to know what this meant. I began making inquiries and never rested until I found a bed-ridden girl praying that

God would bring me to that Church. He had heard her, and brought me over four thousand miles of land and sea in answer to her request."

This story is told in the life of D. L. Moody by his son: but now let me continue it. That girl was a member of my church when I was pastor at New Court. She is still a member, still suffering, still confined to her own room. When in 1901 I was leaving England for America I went to see her. She said to me, "I want you to reach that birthday book." I did so, and turning to February 5 I saw in the handwriting I knew so well, *"D. L. Moody, Psalm 91."* Then Marianne Adlard said to me, "He wrote that for me when he came to see me in 1872, and I prayed for him every day till he went home to God." Continuing, she said, "Now, will you write your name on your birthday page, and let me pray for you until either you or I go home." I shall never forget writing my name in that book. To me the room was full of the Presence. I have often thought of that hour in the rush of busy life, in the place of toil and strain, and even yet by God's good grace I know that Marianne Adlard is praying for me…These are the laborers of force in the fields of God. It is the heroes and heroines who are out of sight, and who labour in prayer, who make it possible for those who are in sight to do their work and win. The force of it to such as are called upon to exercise the ministry can never be measured.

G. Campbell Morgan (1863–1945) was a British Congregational minister serving Westminster, London, for many years. His preaching attracted great crowds, and he was the author of many biblical commentaries and collections of sermons. Biography: Jill Morgan, *A Man of the Word: Life of G. Campbell Morgan* (1951).

More Things Are Wrought by Prayer
Alfred, Lord Tennyson — 1859

More things are wrought by prayer
Than this world dreams of.
Wherefore, let thy voice
Rise like a fountain for me night and day.
For what are men better than sheep and goats
That nourish a blind life within the brain,
If, knowing God, they lift not hands of prayer
Both for themselves and those who call them friend?
For so the whole round earth is every way
Bound by gold chains about the feet of God.

Alfred, Lord Tennyson (1809–1892) was a poet whose work "In Memoriam" and his appointment in 1850 as poet laureate of England established him as the most popular poet of the Victorian era.

Sources

✱

Chapter 1: The Purpose of Prayer

Hallesby, Ole. Reprinted from PRAYER by O. Hallesby, 1931 Augsburg Publishing House [pp. 155–56]. Used by permission of Augsburg Fortress.

Murray, Andrew. *With Christ in the School of Prayer*, 152–55. Grand Rapids: Fleming H. Revell, n.d.

Bunyan, John. *How to Pray in the Spirit*, 15–16. Grand Rapids: Kregel, 1991.

Foster, Richard. Excerpted from pp. 33–4 in PRAYER: FINDING THE HEART'S TRUE HOME by Richard J. Foster. Copyright © 1992 by Richard J. Foster. Reprinted by permission of HarperCollins Publishers Inc.

Underhill, Evelyn. Excerpt is from *Concerning the Inner Life* by Evelyn Underhill (New York: E. P. Dutton & Co. 1926) [pp. 14–18] which is in the Public Domain.

Muller, George. *The Lord's Dealings with George Muller*. London: J. Nisbet and Co.

Dobson, Shirley. Excerpted from *Certain Peace in Uncertain Times* © 2002 by James Dobson, Inc. [pp. 18-20]. Used by permission of Multnomah Publishers, Inc.

Hybels, Bill. Taken from "Too Busy Not to Pray" by Bill Hybels. Copyright © 1998 by Bill Hybels [pp. 7–13]. Used by permission of InterVarsity Press, P.O. Box 1400, Downers Grove, IL 60515. www.ivpress.com.

Willard, Dallas. Taken from "Hearing God" by Dallas Willard. Copyright © 1984, 1993, 1999 by Dallas Willard [pp. 221–22]. Used by permission of InterVarsity Press, P.O. Box 1400, Downers Grove, IL 60515. www.ivpress.com.

Montgomery, James. *Prayer.* N.p., n.d.

Chapter 2: THE PSALMS AS PRAYER

Luther, Martin. "Preface to the Psalter" (1528), *Luther's Works.* In *Word and Sacrament I.* Edited by E. Theodore Bachmann, 254–56. Philadelphia: Muhlenberg Press, 1960.

Law, William. "A Serious Call to a Devout and Holy Life" (1650). In *The Heart of True Spirituality.* Edited by Frank Baker. Grand Rapids: Zondervan, 1985.

Wangerin, Walter, Jr. Taken from WHOLE PRAYER by WALTER WANGERIN JR. Copyright © 1998 by Walter Wangerin Jr. [pp. 53–55]. Used by permission of Zondervan.

Calvin, John. Preface to *Commentary on the Psalms.* Translated by Ford Lewis Battles, 27–29. In *The Piety of John Calvin.* Grand Rapids: Baker, 1978.

Bonhoeffer, Dietrich. From PSALMS: PRAYER BOOK OF THE BIBLE by Dietrich Bonhoeffer, translated by James H. Burtness, copyright © 1970 Augsburg Publishing House [pp. 13–16]. Reprinted by permission of Augsburg Fortress.

Peterson, Eugene H. *Working the Angles,* © 1987 Wm. B. Eerdmans

Publishing Company, Grand Rapids, MI [pp. 32–40]. Used by permission.

Brueggemann, Walter. *Whole Prayer,* 17–20. Winona, Minn.: Saint Mary's Press/Christian Brothers Publications, 1982. Used by permission.

Houston, James. *The Transforming Power of Prayer: Deepening Your Friendship with God,* 108–10. Colorado Springs: NavPress, 1996.

Carmichael, Amy. *Whispers of His Power,* 80. Grand Rapids: Fleming H. Revell, 1982.

Bloom, Anthony. *School of Prayer,* 58–59. London: Darton, Longman and Todd, 1970.

Chapter 3: PATTERNS FOR PRAYER

Guyon, Jeanne. *Experiencing the Depths of Jesus Christ,* 7–11. Beaumont, Tex.: The SeedSowers, n.d.

Luther, Martin. *Luther's Works,* Vol. 43: *Devotional Writings II.* Translated by Carl J. Schindler and edited by Gustav K. Wiencke, 193–95, 198. Philadelphia: Fortress, 1968.

Rinker, Rosalind. *Communicating Love Through Prayer,* 90–95. Grand Rapids: Zondervan, 1966.

Coniaris, Anthony M. *Introducing the Orthodox Church,* 203–204, 206–207. Minneapolis: Light and Life Publications, 1982. Used by permission.

Smith, Martin L. Copyright 1989, Martin L. Smith [pp. 117–21]. All rights reserved. Reprinted from *The Word Is Very Near You* by Martin L. Smith published by Cowley Publications, 907 Massachusetts Ave., Cambridge, MA 02139. www.cowley.org (800-225-1534) [pp. 117–21].

Hybels, Bill. Taken from "Too Busy Not to Pray" by Bill Hybels. Copyright © 1998 by Bill Hybels [pp. 50–59]. Used by permission of InterVarsity Press, P.O. Box 1400, Downers Grove, IL 60515. www.ivpress.com.

Payne, Leanne. *Listening Prayer: Learning to Hear God's Voice and Keep a Prayer Journal,* 19–23. Grand Rapids: Baker, 1994. Used by permission.

Brother Lawrence of the Resurrection. *The Practice of the Presence of God.* Translated by Mary David, 82–85. Westminster, Md.: Newman Book Shop, 1947.

Chapter 4: A Passion for Prayer

Edwards, Jonathan. In *Jonathan Edwards.* Edited by Clarence H. Faust and Thomas H. Johnson, 60–61. New York: American Book Company, n.d.

Louf, André. *Teach Us to Pray: Learning a Little About God.* Translated by Hubert Hoskins, 44–45. Boston: Cowley, 1974.

Tada, Joni Eareckson. Excerpted from *A Quiet Place in a Crazy World* © 1993 by Joni Eareckson Tada [pp. 113–15]. Used by permission of Multnomah Publishers, Inc.

Foster, Richard J. Excerpted from pp. 3–4 in PRAYER: FINDING THE HEART'S TRUE HOME by Richard J. Foster. Copyright © 1992 by Richard J. Foster. Reprinted by permission of HarperCollins Publishers Inc.

Kelly, Thomas R. *A Testament of Devotion,* 35–40. New York: Harper and Brothers, 1941.

Murray, Andrew. *With Christ in the School of Prayer,* 32–37. New York: Fleming H. Revell.

Hansen, David. Taken from "Long Wandering Prayer" by David

Hansen. Copyright © 2001 by David Hansen [91–94]. Used by permission of InterVarsity Press, P.O. Box 1400, Downers Grove, IL 60515. www.ivpress.com.

Bounds, E. M. *Purpose in Prayer,* 58–60. Old Tappan, N.J.: Fleming H. Revell, 1920.

Watts, Isaac. *Isaac Watt's Guide to Prayer.* Abridged and edited by Harry Escott, 25–28 London: Epworth, 1948.

Omartian, Stormie. Taken from: *The Power of a Praying Parent* by Stormie Omartian. Copyright © 1995 by Harvest House Publishers, Eugene, OR 97402 [pp. 18–22]. Used by permission.

Wesley, Charles. Verses from "Soldiers of Christ, Arise" (1749). Quoted from *English Spirituality in the Age of Wesley.* Edited by David Lyle Jeffrey, 274–75. Grand Rapids: Eerdmans, 1987.

Chapter 5: THE POSTURE OF PRAYER

Cedar, Paul. *A Life of Prayer: Cultivating the Inner Life of the Christian Leader,* 60–62. Nashville: Thomas Nelson, 1998. Used by permission of Thomas Nelson, Inc.

Taylor, Jeremy. *Holy Living.* Edited by P. G. Stanwood, 215–16. Oxford: Clarendon, 1989.

Tugwell, Simon. *Prayer in Practice,* by Simon Tugwell, Templegate Publishers (templegate.com), 1974 [pp. 27–32]. Used by permission.

Smith, Martin L. *The Word Is Very Near You,* 81–82, 88–90. Cambridge, Mass.: Cowley, 1989.

Merrill, Dean. "Whatever Happened to Kneeling?" *Christianity Today,* 24. 10 February 1992. Copyright 1992 by Dean Merrill. Reprinted with permission.

Miller, Calvin. *Into the Depths of God,* 153–55. Minneapolis: Bethany House, 2000. Used by permission.

Griffin, Emilie. *Doors into Prayer: An Invitation*, 28–29. Brewster, Mass.: Paraclete, 2001.

Thompson, Marjorie J. From *Family, the Forming Center*. Copyright © 1996 by Marjorie J. Thompson [pp. 76–77]. Used by permission of Upper Room Books.

Lewis, C. S. *The Screwtape Letters*, 19–20. New York: Macmillan, 1961.

Chapter 6: Problems with Prayer

Nouwen, Henri. *Springs of Hope*. New York: Bantam Books, 1989.

Torrey, R. A. *Hindrances to Prayer*, 66–76. Chicago: Moody Press, 1976. Used by permission.

Willard, Dallas. *Hearing God: Developing a Conversational Relationship with God*, 217–19. Downers Grove, Ill.: InterVarsity, 1999.

Fosdick, Harry Emerson. *The Meaning of Prayer*, 81–83. New York: Young Men's Christian Association, 1915.

Myers, Ruth, with Warren Myers. Excerpted from *31 Days of Prayer* © 1997 by Warren and Ruth Myers. Used by permission of Multnomah Publishers, Inc. [pp. 193–96].

Hansen, David. Taken from "Long Wandering Prayer" by David Hansen. Copyright © 2001 by David Hansen [pp. 27–28, 131–32]. Used by permission of InterVarsity Press, P. O. Box 1400, Downers Grove, IL 60515. www.ivpress.com

Hallesby, Ole. Reprinted from PRAYER by O. Hallesby, 1931 Augsburg Publishing House [pp. 113–15]. Used by permission of Augsburg Fortress.

Gaddy, C. Welton. *A Love Affair with God: Finding Freedom and Intimacy in Prayer*, 146, 152–53. Nashville: Broadman and Holman, 1995. Used by permission.

Dodd, Brian J. Taken from "Praying Jesus' Way" by Brian Dodd.

Copyright © 1997 by Brian J. Dodd [pp. 57–60]. Used by permission of InterVarsity Press, P.O. Box 1400, Downers Grove, IL 60515. www.ivpress.com.

Chapter 7: POWERLESSNESS AND PRAYER

Bunyan, John. *How to Pray in the Spirit*, 103–104. Grand Rapids: Kregel, 1991.

Calvin, John. *Institution of the Christian Religion* (1536). Translated by Ford Lewis Battles, 92–95. In *The Piety of John Calvin*. Grand Rapids: Baker, 1978.

Nouwen, Henri. Excerpted from *With Open Hands* by Henri J. M. Nouwen. Copyright ©1972, 1995 by Ave Maria Press, P.O. Box 428, Notre Dame, IN 46556, www.avemariapress.com [pp. 51, 54]. Used with permission of the publisher.

Houston, James. *The Transforming Power of Prayer: Deepening Your Friendship with God*, 122–27. Colorado Springs: NavPress, 1996.

Chan, Simon. *Spiritual Theology: A Systematic Study of the Christian Life*, 134–36. Downers Grove, Ill.: InterVarsity, 1998.

Mother Teresa. In *Seeking the Heart of God: Reflections on Prayer*. By Mother Teresa and Brother Roger, 13–14. San Francisco: HarperSanFrancisco, 1991.

Sanders, J. Oswald. *Prayer Power Unlimited: Achieving Intimacy with God through Prayer*, 64–70. Palo Alto, Calif.: Discovery House, 1997.

Carmichael, Amy. *Edges of His Ways*, 195–97. London: S.P.C.K., 1955.

Chapter 8: PUBLIC AND PRIVATE PRAYER

Wangerin, Walter, Jr. Taken from **WHOLE PRAYER** by WALTER WANGERIN JR. Copyright © 1998 by Walter Wangerin Jr. [pp. 77–79, 85]. Used by permission of Zondervan.

Finney, Charles G. *Principles of Prayer,* 106–107, 114–15. Minneapolis: Bethany House, 2001. Used by permission.

Calvin, John. *Institution of the Christian Religion* (1536). Translated by Ford Lewis Battles, 98–100. *The Piety of John Calvin.* Grand Rapids: Baker, 1978.

Cymbala, Jim. Taken from FRESH WIND, FRESH FIRE by JIM CYMBALA; DEAN MERRILL. Copyright © 1997 by Jim Cymbala [pp. 27–30]. Used by permission of Zondervan.

Buttrick, George A. *Prayer,* 249–50. New York: Abingdon-Cokesbury, 1942.

Oden, Thomas C. Pages 99–102 from PASTORAL THEOLOGY: ESSENTIALS OF MINISTRY by THOMAS C. ODEN. Copyright © 1983 by Thomas C. Oden. Reprinted by permission of HarperCollins Publishers Inc.

Peterson, Eugene H. *Earth and Altar,* Downers Grove, Ill.: InterVarsity, 1985.

Merton, Thomas. From NEW SEEDS OF CONTEMPLATION, copyright ©1961 by The Abbey of Gethsemani, Inc. [pp. 80–83]. Reprinted by permission of New Directions Publishing Corp.

Chapter 9: PASTORAL PRAYER

Bounds, E. M. *The Weapon of Prayer.* Old Tappan, N.J.: Fleming H. Revell, 1931. Reprint ed., 103–105, 109, 111. Grand Rapids: Baker, 1975.

Oden, Thomas C. Pages 89–90 from PASTORAL THEOLOGY: ESSENTIALS OF MINISTRY by THOMAS C. ODEN. Copyright © 1983 by Thomas C. Oden. Reprinted by permission of HarperCollins Publishers Inc.

Frye, John W. Taken from JESUS THE PASTOR by JOHN W. FRYE.

Copyright © 2000 by John W. Frye [pp. 139, 164–65]. Used by permission of Zondervan.

Buttrick, George A. *Prayer,* 283–85, 292. New York: Abingdon-Cokesbury, 1942.

Willimon, William H. From *Pastor: The Theology and Practice of Ordained Ministry* © 2002 by Abingdon Press [pp. 82–83]. Used by permission.

Dodd, Brian J. Taken from "Praying Jesus' Way" by Brian Dodd. Copyright © 1997 by Brian J. Dodd [pp. 116–19]. Used by permission of InterVarsity Press, P.O. Box 1400, Downers Grove, IL 60515. www.ivpress.com

Foster, Richard J. Excerpted from pp. 208–9 in PRAYER: FINDING THE HEART'S TRUE HOME by Richard J. Foster. Copyright © 1992 by Richard J. Foster. Reprinted by permission of HarperCollins Publishers Inc.

Murray, Andrew. *Divine Healing,* 123–25. Minneapolis: Bethany, 2002.

MacNutt, Francis. Excerpted from *Healing: Silver Anniversary Edition* by Francis MacNutt, Ph.D. Copyright ©1974, 1999 by Ave Maria Press, P.O. Box 428, Notre Dame, IN, 46556, www.avemariapress.com [pp. 161–64]. Used with permission of the publisher. 161–64.

Griffin, Emilie. *Doors into Prayer: An Invitation,* 87–88. Brewster, Mass.: Paraclete, 2001.

Chapter 10: THE POWER OF PRAYER

Chambers, Oswald. This material is taken from *My Utmost for His Highest* by Oswald Chambers, edited by James Reinmann, copyright © 1992 by Oswald Chambers Publications Assn., Ltd.

Original edition copyright © 1935 by Dodd Mead & Co., renewed 1963 by the Oswald Chambers Publications Assn., Ltd., and is used by permission of Discovery House Publishers, Box 3566, Grand Rapids MI 49501. All rights reserved.

Gordon, S. D. *Quiet Talks on Prayer,* 9–10. New York: Fleming H. Revell, 1904.

Edwards, Jonathan. *Apocalyptic Writings.* Edited by Stephen J. Stein, 355–57. New Haven, Conn.: Yale University, 1977.

Spurgeon, Charles. *The Power of Prayer in a Believer's Life,* 94–96. Lynnwood, Wash.: Emerald Books, 1993.

Lucado, Max. *He Still Moves Stone* by Max Lucado, copyright © 1993, W Publishing Group, Nashville, Tennessee [pp. 97–101]. All rights reserved. Used by permission.

Peterson, Eugene H. *Where Your Treasure Is,* ©1985 Eugene H. Peterson, current edition published 1993 by Wm. B. Eerdmans Publishing Company, Grand Rapids, MI. Used by permission.

Bounds, E. M. *Purpose in Prayer,* 9–11. New York: Fleming H. Revell, 1920.

Evans, Tony. *The Battle Is the Lord's,* 315–17. Chicago: Moody Press, 1998. Used by permission.

Stafford, Tim. Excerpted from *Knowing the Face of God* by Tim Stafford. Copyright 1986 [pp. 134–36]. Used by permission of NavPress—www.navpress.com. All rights reserved.

Morgan, G. Campbell. *The Practice of Prayer,* 125–27. Reprint ed., Grand Rapids: Baker, 1971.

Tennyson, Alfred, Lord. "Morte D'Arthur." From *The Poetical Works of Alfred, Lord Tennyson.* Edited by Eugene Parsons, 78. New York: Thomas Y. Crowell, 1897.

Printed in the United States
By Bookmasters